# TACKLE GOLF

# Tackle Golf

**JOHN STOBBS**

**STANLEY PAUL**
*London*

STANLEY PAUL & CO LTD
3 Fitzroy Square, London W1

An imprint of the Hutchinson Publishing Group

London Melbourne Sydney Auckland
Wellington Johannesburg Cape Town
and agencies throughout the world

First published 1961
Second impression 1965
This edition 1968
Revised edition 1975

Printed in Great Britain by offset litho by
The Anchor Press Ltd, and bound by
Wm Brendon & Son Ltd, both of Tiptree, Essex

ISBN 0 09 123840 4 (cased)
0 09 123841 2 (paperback)

*To my father, J. L. Stobbs*

who told me, when I was eight years old: 'You just have to stand in the right way and grip the club in the right way, and then simply swing. . . .'

# Contents

# Illustrations

# Author's Note

Almost every golf book ever read offers some new idea, or some new way of putting an old idea. But I should like to acknowledge a particular debt to the following writers of analytical or instructional books or articles:

*Professional:* The late Harry Vardon; J. H. Taylor, Henry Cotton, Ernest Jones, John Jacobs, and (with Herbert Warren Wind) Ben Hogan.

*Amateur:* The late H. S. C. Everard; Roger Wethered, Joyce Wethered, R. T. Jones Jnr., Bernard Darwin, Henry Longhurst.

Above all, my most cordial thanks to all my fellow addicts at Berkhamsted, not only for hundreds of enjoyable rounds in their company but also for splendidly illustrating the wider possibilities of the game and how to enjoy it.

# Introduction

'Tackle golf . . .' It's what we've all been trying to do for years: in my case, for forty. And if there's one thing you very soon find out about golf it is that you can never have it really pinned down. Even the greatest champions produce the sorriest of strokes; and no man has ever won the Open without playing one or two palpably bad ones. Champions expect it. Unlike (to take an obvious example) great pianists, they know that every so often they will hit a plainly 'wrong note',

This is because no amount of method, practice, and determination can guard anyone in golf against the momentary aberration. It is a slow-motion game, in that each stroke is an entirely separate exercise in itself. 'The ball maun still be hit,' as someone in the mythology of the game said once; and it is not in the nature of man to function entirely as a machine. His state of mind is bound up closely with each stroke; and his mind is not that of a 100 per cent repeating electronic calculator; it is a highly sensitive *initiating* agent, providing in itself 'programme', data, calculation, motive power, and application of results. Throughout its working, extraneous information is trying to gum up the works; delight at what he has done already, fear of a bad stroke or of a particular hazard, doubt about tactics, indigestion, a peculiar irrational feeling of being uncomfortable on a particular address, movements in the gallery, photographers, the half-sight of a pretty wench, even (as that realist amongst golf maniacs P. G. Wodehouse put it) 'the uproar of the butterflies in the adjoining meadows', can all throw a particular stroke that 5 per cent out of line or balance which makes all the difference to the result.

Looked at as a mental calculation followed by a mechanical

application, a really good golf shot is something of an unlikely feat. It is in the game's character as an exposition of human talent and capability that half its fascination lies.

It is also a game in which, in the ultimate resource, a man can only help himself. This book is an attempt to help him, in its turn, to do so.

It is not meant in any way as a substitute for professional tuition and advice. On the contrary, it assumes that the 'tackler', whether he be a complete beginner or an established player, will go to his club professional for what no book in the world can ever supply—the practical on-the-spot analysis of what he is *actually* doing, as opposed to what he thinks he is doing. It also assumes that anyone taking up the game will begin by learning from the pro the easiest grip, stance, and general approach to the shot.

No professional in the world, though, can give you your best game out of his shop: you can only take his basic instruction and then build up your own method upon it, going back to him regularly for a check-up on how you are developing.

What this book aims to do is to chart what seems to me to be the easiest course through what has now become something of a jungle of golf theory and analysis (not without an occasional warning of 'Here be dragons!'), to set out as simply as possible the secrets of hitting the ball to one's own satisfaction, and to give some guide to how a player may work out for himself its subtleties, its complications, and its quite inordinate possibilities for enjoyment.

I

# First temptation!

Right then. Let's assume you have the clubs and the balls and are ready to play the game with all the will in the world.

How to start?

The moment of greatest danger is upon you—especially if you have been a cricketer, tennis player, or hockey enthusiast, and/or have a natural aptitude and eye for games. The first fairway stretches invitingly before you. You have chosen a moment when few players are about. The temptation to tee up the ball and take a swipe at it is overwhelming.

Of course it is. Go ahead then. Wallop it. Round the whole course if you like.

Well done! Three balls left! Just a matter of concentration—getting the knack—looking at it carefully—you'll soon be hitting it.

Now this is precisely the danger. You *will* soon be hitting it—as like as not quite well.

THIS IS THE MOMENT TO STOP. There are three million ways of hitting a golf ball, and you have already discovered some score of them. Go on, and you'll soon be playing round with other golfers; you'll be getting better and better at it; your first good drive, or bogey—or even a hole in one—will whet your appetite for more and greater trial and error. Within a year you'll be irredeemable.

The courses of Britain are crowded with men and women who have never got themselves right from the start. They have condemned themselves to be duffers, more or less, for the remainder of their golfing days. They have also condemned themselves to most of the minor ills and irritations—sprained wrists, creaky backs, cartilages—which doing anything both energetically and awkwardly sooner or later, but probably later, brings on.

Any old wrong way works after a fashion. But it very soon becomes part of your mind, your bodily habit, your whole approach to the game. It makes the game the more difficult, the more successful you get. And it puts firm limits on your progress and enjoyment.

*Now is the moment to go to the Pro!*

2

# What the Professional can do for you

It is one of the eternally startling things about golf how shy the genuine beginner—and often the experienced but not-so-successful golfer—is about approaching his professional. After all, he is there for you, and for no one if not for you!

It is not just his business to sell you the clubs and balls and clothes and equipment which may catch your eye in his shop. It is intensely his interest to help you to play and enjoy the game. He is not just a professor for the more advanced students. He is the master of the elementary class. Introduce yourself. Tell him what stage you have reached—if any at all. Ask about lessons.

Don't be put off, or hurt, if he hands you over to one of his assistants. They are there not just to help him in the shop, and to learn their profession from him, but to practise it. Any of them can put you on the right road from the beginning. Later on, the professional himself can take you over, as you progress.

Read even several good instructional books first, by all means, if you care to. But *you are an individual case.* You will make *individual* mistakes and misinterpretations of the written word, or the printed photograph. You may also need to be started off on some lines not exactly identical with the most common methods amongst the best players. Part of the fascination of his practice to a golf professional is that human beings come in all shapes, sizes, types of physical structure, and temperaments; and the advice must fit the player. If, for instance, you hear from another beginner that the pro has told him something quite different from what he has told you, or given him a different grip or stance, don't be surprised—or suspicious. It is quite common for an advanced teaching-professional to give entirely contradictory advice to scratch-men who to you would look identical in their methods. The pro can spot the nuances, can see where errors of swing *begin*, and has learned from long experience how the thoughts in the mind can affect the movements of different people's bodies in quite contrasting ways.

You are a unique case. If your professional is worthy of his salt, he will treat you as one.

It would be a waste of time entirely for me to specify here the very first steps in grip and stance, etc., through which he will take you. But almost at once in your golfing career you will notice that a very large proportion of golfers have never been to him, and have never learned the basic fundamentals of all good golfing method. If anything he tells you, or anything in the chapters which follow, seems to contradict what you see on the course—then watch carefully and observe how well what you see seems to work! Those who do not prove the rule do not often— I'll warrant—go round in less than 80. There *are* exceptions (and beware of them!) even amongst some of the best professionals in the world; but they are rare and individual ones. Nevertheless, it's only fair to emphasize that the right grip, the right stance, and the right approach to the shot ('setting-up' as the professional will probably call it), are probably more important than anything else in golf; in this sense: that any errors in them make everything else just that little bit more difficult than it needs to be. Let the professional know that you mean to get these fundamentals as right as his; then go back to him regularly after your first lessons and ask him to give you a critical look-over as you hit a few shots. Grip, stance, and 'setting-up' all go wrong regularly of their own accord, especially as a longer-handicap man's game develops.

If you don't get them right from the beginning it will be much more difficult—and inconvenient—to get them right later on.

At this point, the writer intrudes (with all apologies) in his working capacity, for a moment!

When I originally had the colossal presumption to accept the invitation to write this book, pages 16 and 17 took in two lengthy and detailed photograph captions. The position of the photographs have been changed for this Revised edition and so I find myself with a page and a quarter of space to fill, and most certainly a very great deal more could be said about the sad neglect by most week-end golfers of their professional's ability to help them.

All too often, the poor chap has to listen patiently while they call upon Inscrutiable Providence to tell them what on earth they're doing wrong (and why they're in the bushes again), when he's bursting to tell them himself—and to help them to have more fun at the game!

They even come beefing into his shop about what a wretched time they've had on the course, and expect him to be sympathetic —when they never ever ask his help about it!

Over golf's years, I've pondered a lot about why club golfers don't seek their Pro's help more. I suspect it boils down to two main reasons.

*First*: most golfers really are far too modest, even to themselves, about what they really are capable of on the course.

*Second*: Most men, anyway, far far prefer worrying anything out for themselves, than seeking anyone else's advice about it. (We all instinctively, and usually bolshily, hate being told we've got something all wrong.)

This is, of course, part of the Briton's proud, proper, excellent, independent, individualistic, self-reliant, bloody-minded determination to do everything his own way, on his own authority, and not anyone else's. This is our breed (all 57 varieties of it), and our national tradition (all 17 versions of them) alike.

So here's one way of finding a useful compromise; by which any man (or woman) can still make the most excellent use of his professional's skill to assist in a very simple way indeed.

Nearly all club professionals are accomplished and accurate mimics. So why not ask yours to show you what your swing looks like, to *you* as you watch?

He can show you, watching *him*, exactly how the bad shots you want to avoid begin, in your case: and exactly how they work.

He doesn't have to talk to you much about it. He can just *show* you what; whence; how; what result. He can even hit shots for you exactly like your bugbears; and demonstrate to you which kinds of error go inevitably with which others, and exactly how the mechanics of them work.

You yourself can then apply all he shows you, quite independently, to your own swing, in your own way.

It does work! In truth, it's the *only* sure way to make the best of whatever game we may have in us.

(With which probably brutal thought, the writer apologizes for intruding. Original edition; please take over again!)

# 3

# How the ball is hit

It isn't!

It is swept, clipped, pushed, or tapped.

'Pushed' may surprise you, but the better a player gets at the game the greater proportion of his strokes are putts across the green at or into the hole. There are many ways of playing the putt. One of them is the stiff-wristed push straight through the ball; another is the simple sharp tap or rap. And that we can now leave until we turn to putting in a later chapter.

'Clipped' is a word I use myself to describe something which

real (one could almost say secret) essence of nearly all the
:r shots in the game. It is seen and felt in its purest forms in
and-action on short shots with iron clubs. It is the way in
h the club-head clips the ball on to and away from its
hitting-face, as it is swung the last few inches towards the
bottom-dead-centre of the swing.

You can 'clip' a ball in cleanest and purest timing with a
swing coming almost entirely from the hands and forearms alone
—and indeed you will find yourself doing so in advanced chip
shots later on. And even when you are playing a longer iron shot
over some 150 yards or so, with a full swing that sweeps the club-
head through the ball, the essence of the clipping action will
still be there, if the shot is to be a true, well-timed, and accurate
one.

### The simplest golf shot in the world

If you want to understand this fundamental straight away, take
your 7-iron. Hold it the way the pro has shown you. Now swing
it back a couple of feet, letting the face turn away from the ball
naturally, and then swing it smoothly forward through the ball
*to slide through the grass two inches in front of the ball, but directly
opposite your hands.*

A clip. Almost a snip. A sweet touch. A little bound up and
forward from the ball, as the club-face takes it neatly away and
then completes the little swing to two feet or so beyond the ball.

There you have straight away the essence of all good method
in iron shots. The club-face picks up the ball on the last stage of
the downward arc, fractionally before the arc passes through the
surface of the grass, before continuing evenly on and away from
the grass again.

Before, before, before, *before* it touches the ground.

And *before* it catches up to a line level with the hands, as they
swing in their smaller arc from the shoulders.

There is no hit *at* the ball at all. There is simply a swinging of
the club-head smoothly and evenly through the surface of the
grass. The bottom-dead-centre of the arc, through which the
club-head is swung, needs to be an inch or two inches in front of
the ball, so that the ball is—*quite incidentally*—picked up by the

club-head and clipped forward, just before the club-head swings through that bottom-dead-centre.[1]

There is nothing complicated about this; but it is the key to all good scoring. Above all, because it is the little shot which will put the ball close to the hole from just off the smooth putting surface of the green.

You can prove this to yourself. Practise it on the practice ground, just sending the ball ten yards or so. It should rise no more than a foot to a couple of feet above the ground (if it rises more, then your hands are not swinging ahead of *and with* the club-head), and you should be able to see that (or sense that) the ball is spinning backwards towards you slightly as it takes a little bound away.

When you can vary the strength of the clip to send the ball anything from ten to twenty yards, try it out on the practice green, or—if practice on the course is allowed, as it is on nine out of ten courses—on to one of the actual greens.

This shot you can now spend the rest of your golfing life practising!

If you are a true week-end golfer you will never find yourself hitting every green from longer distances in every round. In fact, the best players in the world never do so either. Your scoring, and your rating in the game, will depend tremendously on your being able to clip the ball neatly and smoothly up to within two feet of the edge of the hole from any fairly decent lie round the green.

Get good at it, and you have the basic 'chip-shot' under your command.

You will also have laid the basis of every iron shot in the bag. How much arm-swing, and slight hip-lead into the stroke, you combine with it is entirely up to you. So whether you prefer to clip it up with a small throw-through of the club-head, towards the hole, or to clip it low with a more pronounced leading movement of the hands (keeping them more in front of the position of the club-head, so that they partly drag it through the ball), is

[1] I use this phrase to describe the point at which the club-shaft passes through a vertical plane—the moment at which, viewed from in front of the player, it looks at right angles to the ground.

also entirely up to you. The best advice you could take is to ask if you may watch your professional at chipping practice; and note how he varies the movement slightly to make the ball do different things.

Some people find it a great help to try aiming at a point on the grass, 'in front of the ball, and just swinging the club-head to connect with the grass there—automatically picking up the ball on the way.

The professional can really *show* you how to do it. I'm just trying to put the idea as clearly as possible into your head. I do suggest that you tackle this first.

# 4

# Variations on the simple chip

### Arms and hands

I'm sorry. Teeing up a ball and womping at it with a driver or other wooden club comes later. (It comes later, anyway, as far as this system of tackling golf is concerned!) There is a logic in the building of golfing craftsmanship; and there are many different types of strokes to learn about and have fun with. The longer shots are a different proposition entirely from the basis of the week-end golfers' scoring—which is getting the ball to the green and into the hole.

Back, then, to the little chip shots you are now getting the hang of, and clipping neatly off the grass on to the green and up to the hole.

You will already have discovered that you can make them fly at different heights, *for the same length of shot*, and that sometimes the ball seems to bound forward on landing, and sometimes it pulls up fairly quickly. Why does this happen and how can you turn it to your own enjoyment?

There are two factors here. First the swing itself.

In more or less any shot in golf there are two swings rolled into one. One is the swing of your arms around your spine. The other is the swinging movement of the club-head around the hands, which is in practice superimposed on the swing of the arms themselves. It is almost entirely this latter 'hand-action' swing that you have been practising on your chip shots.

You will have noticed, though, that you have been instinctively swinging your hands around your upper spine (via your arms and shoulders) as you played them (or I hope you have, for you would be frightfully uncomfortable if you didn't). The next stage is to work out by experiment and practice how you can produce different types of shots by different variations of these two swings-within-the-swing.

Try experimenting with this as a generalization: *The point at which the hand-action swing of the club-head catches up with the shoulder-action swing of the hands determines how high the ball will fly for any particular club.*

### 'Hitting early'

If, for example, the club-head catches up with the hands just *before* the ball is clipped by the face, then the shot will be a high one (if it makes proper contact at all!); in this case, bottom-dead-centre of the two swings coincides just behind or just under the ball, and the club-face is travelling horizontally as it passes through the ball.

Think about this for a moment. First, you will get maximum effect (for a straight hit) of the loft on the club. Second, if you try to do it when the ball is in a bad lie, or when there is a little lump on the ground behind it, you will probably hit the ground before the ball—and fluff the shot.

Unless the ball is teed up (either on a peg tee, or naturally perched in grass) and he wants exceptional height from the shot, a good golfer hardly ever moves the bottom of his swing further back than that. By this I mean he hardly ever brings in the hand-action swing even earlier, so that the club-head has passed ahead of the hands by the time it clips the ball. Even when he seems to, he will almost certainly get this effect by moving the whole vertical axis of his swing backwards at any angle away from the target—so that in effect he is using his normal timing, but swinging slightly upwards.

He may do this on a drive, if he wants exceptional height with a wind behind him for maximum length. He may do it on a chip if he has to clear a highish obstacle, like a mound. But he will certainly always avoid bringing in the hand-action early whenever possible—for it is a dangerous and difficult method of striking a golf ball!

The fact that it is both dangerous and difficult does not deter 75 per cent of really bad golfers from doing it most of the time— or trying to. Hence the flying divots, the sclaffs,[1] and the general unhappiness of the man who can't seem to get the ball in the air, however high he tries to hit it.

The technical name for it is 'hitting early'—in other words, throwing your hand-action swing through in advance of your body-and-arm action.

Back, then, to chipping; now *Example* 2.

### 'Hitting late'

If the club-head catches up with the hands *fractionally after* the ball is clipped, then you get the normal stroke. Both hand-swing and arm-swing hit their respective bottom-dead-centres as the ball is beginning its journey. This is the one you have been practising, and it is the most important one.

*Example 3*, though, is also worth practising. It is used for two purposes, clearest in chipping and shorter approaches. This is when the hand-action swing of the club-head is timed to come in *late* in relation to the body-and-arm swing. In this case the hands have already swung to a position definitely in front of (or past) the ball before the club-head is swung through the ball towards its own bottom-dead-centre, clipping the ball up on its way.

The club-head may then catch up with the hands definitely in front of the ball; or, if you choose to play an even lower-flying 'dragged' shot, it may not catch up with the hands until even some twelve inches after the ball is clipped. The characteristics of this sort of shot are a very crisp, biting sort of clip of the ball;

[1] A foozle resulting from hitting the ground behind the ball, or digging under it.

**Here's the perfect golf shot: a rotary swing in action**

Grace, brains, balance, precision mechanics, timing: all relaxed into the making of a perfect golf shot. Vivien Saunders; B.Sc. (Psychology) Professional Golfer, shows just how simple golf is: hands *leading* clubhead into her swing's bottom-dead-centre for a finesse-clean bunker shot.

Vivien Saunders: *Peter Dazeley*

**Golf is a rotary movement all the way through**

You can *only* play good golf happily by swinging your arms, hands and clubhead in one rhythmic connected flow; timed to discharge the clubhead's momentum into a smooth-flowing movement *through* the ball – *not* just project it *at* it!

This swing of the arms and clubhead actually *revolves around* a point in the player's upper chest. But a better way for the player to

think of it is of working his swing around a centre point of gravity
which balances weight and position of body, with momentum of and
centrifugal force in, arms and clubhead.

This any player can only *feel*, as that centre which holds him in
balance, right through the shot; and from which he can best
discharge momentum smoothly outwards into clubhead acceleration
through the ball, and on up into the follow-through.

Tom Weiskopf: *Peter Dazeley*/Peter Oosterhuis: *H. W. Neale*

**Even this sort of shot is easy!**

Vivien Saunders, again: cutting one up off a steep down-slope, to
fly high up over the bunker (bound to be there), then stop sharply
by the pin. The secret? Swing (and bottom-dead centre) alike
angled parallel with the slope: with an open club face cutting the
ball sharply upwards as it swings down and forward. Note the
hands: well *in front of* where the ball lay.

Vivien Saunders: *Peter Dazeley*

a low flight *for the club used*; an increased backspin effect on the ball, which counteracts the tendency to greater run from the lower shot; and a larger divot taken out of the ground in front of the ball—since the club-head is still swinging slightly downwards as it takes the ball.

Before leaving this point, note that you have only to carry this sequence a little further and you have the 'chop' shot, which you will find useful for hacking the ball desperately out of thick grass, or really bad lies. But this stroke belongs in the category of recovery shots; and we'll be going into them later.

That's all there is to basic chipping.

It may sound very difficult and complicated to the beginner (or even to some others). But it isn't. These different sorts of chips are not impositions laid upon the aspiring golfer by the austruse mechanics of the game. They are merely tools for his enjoyment. Nor are they all exact types of chips to be rigidly adhered to, and rigidly separated. They all run into one another, and can be combined. A drag shot can be hit slightly earlier; a high-lofted floater slightly later. The thing is to get the feel of the various combinations and movements, note their effects *as you do them*; and then practise and experiment happily away until this basic golfing dexterity begins to become instinctive.

It will, remarkably quickly. You will soon find that you will not be looking at a chip or approach shot (the higher-flying ones are called 'pitches') and trying to work out which system of movements you need to use. You will simply be deciding what sort of little flight, bounce, and run you want on the ball, and how much backspin to grip the green; and then you will just play the shot. It's as simple as writing a sentence; your mind tells you the words you want and you just write them. You don't have to work them out letter by letter, as you did once when you were first learning to read and write.

### Aim and stance

One thing to be careful of, though. Whatever shot you choose to play you must so set the club-head and so work the hands that the club-face aims towards the hole both as you address the ball and as you hit it.

The eye can deceive here. If you find you can't hit the shots straight, then you are probably not lining up the club-face straight in the first place.

The *markings on the face* must always be at right angles to the direction you want the ball to go.

You will find it helpful, too, if you experiment with different stances and ball positions. Most good golfers (but not all) find that it helps to place the hands at the address in the position in relation to the ball that they want to have at impact. As a corollary, if the shot is to be high then the ball wants to be forward, nearer a line to the left toe. If the shot is going to be hit late and flighted low, then the ball rests more comfortably nearly opposite the right toe. Other shots between the two.

Many good golfers also find that chip shots are more easily played if the left foot is drawn back a bit from the line right-toe-to-pin. Many also find that the right foot is best set at right angles to that same line, with the left turned or opened slightly towards the direction of the shot. How much is entirely a matter of how you prefer it—as, of course, is much else in golf.

Don't, above all, tense up. The professional will have told you already that this is one of the basics of general grip and stance. With chipping it is truer than anywhere. Knees should be comfortably relaxed, elbows relaxed as much as you like.

Above all: the chip is a *swing*. Don't *hit* the ball towards the pin; *swing* the club-head and let the ball be *incidentally* clipped away.

### Strength of shot and 'feel'

Strength is instinct. Instinct is experience accumulated. Sorry, but no short cuts at all! Only practice can give it to you.

When you get it, it will come as 'feel'. It will express itself above all through the sensitivity of the forefinger of the right hand, localized in and around the inside of the middle joint of the finger. Unless that finger is crooked delicately around the shaft, with the knuckle on top of the shaft and the finger-tip below it, you are unlikely ever to be a master of touch and feel on chips.

The professional (especially if you are a beginner) may have given you personally a grip with the right hand which keeps the top knuckle of the right forefinger rather behind than above the shaft. That is for general play. In chipping and all delicate little shots around the green you are at liberty to try moving it over to the left a bit. You will find that many of the best players in the world use an entirely different grip for putting—which is a thing a man is free to choose. You are at complete liberty to vary your grip a little for chipping too.

You will never chip well with the 'touch' operating via the palm or thumb-pad of your right hand; you are likely to chip your best via the crook of the forefinger, or via the third pad from the tip of it, or—most likely—both combined.

If it doesn't seem to work, try different positions of your left hand. Some chip well with the left hand turned to the right and rather over the top of the shaft, or with the back of the hand looking rather flat on top of the shaft. Some people find it better to turn it outwards round the grip so that only one knuckle is visible, and the backs of the hand and wrist face towards the hole.

Don't try and hit the ball up. Swing forward, slightly down, and through—and let the club-head clip the ball away.

# 5

# Moving into the irons

I suggest you approach iron shots from the bottom end. Instead of learning how to hit a 2-iron shot 220 yards, take off from the point you have already reached—a command of the various methods and craftsmanships of chipping. Move gradually further and further away from your aiming point (for things now must continue on the practice ground); first to 50 yards, then 75, then 100, then 150. At each stage practise until you begin to feel you have command of the shot, and play whichever type of stroke you choose, to end at the point aimed at.

Play them all in amongst each other. For instance, when playing to seventy-five yards don't keep playing shot after shot of the ordinary pitch variety with a wedge, 9-iron, or 8-iron. Play one to fly high and stop quickly. Play another low, with run (all with the same club). Try them with different clubs—for each has its variations of possibility. Go out in a wind and play them in all directions, against, or across, the wind and note how you personally can best adjust your method to its effects. (Many experts will tell you, by the way, that a perfectly hit shot is not affected by wind, except in its length of travel. This I have always doubted. But opinions always vary in golf.)

You will soon find that a cut-up sort of shot (tending to fly high and curve right) is murder—unless very well controlled—in a left-hand wind. And a slightly hooked one (bending towards the left) is equally ruinous in a right-hand wind.

For the rest you can work on just *naturally* extending the movements you used in chipping. Here are some notes which may help:

1. *Swing* hands and club together. The secondary hand-action which swings the club-head itself, and gives the main touch and control on chips and short pitches, becomes progressively less important-seeming as the range gets longer. It isn't really, of course, since timing and action can only come from the hands, and indeed still from that forefinger of your right hand. But since sending a ball further and further calls for a longer and longer, and stronger and stronger, body-and-arm swing, then *consciousness* of the hand-action becomes less and less: and the whole thing can become more of a 'one-piece' affair.

2. The *arc* of the swing begins to count more and more as the shot gets longer and longer. In chipping you can get away with anything, so long as your hands bring the club-head through the ball in the right way. You could even play all chip shots with your legs crossed, and still become an exceptionally efficient chipper. But the longer the shot becomes, the greater will be the effects, in direction, of any swinging of the club in anything but a straight line through the ball.

This straight line covers just the part twelve inches or so through impact, and most of the twelve inches—remember—represents the very bottom of the sweep of the swing *after* the club-head has clipped into the ball.

If you put a whitewash line along the ground, passing through the ball towards the target, then the club must be swung *inside* that on the back *and* on the down-swing, and must eventually go inside it again on the through-swing (called from now on by its proper name the 'follow-through'). Imagine that the path of the club-head travels along the rim of a curve[1] described around the point in your spine at the back of your shoulders. If that point was vertically above the ball when you addressed it, then this curve would be standing on its edge in the vertical plane, and covering the white line throughout.

But it is not. The curve of the swing is cocked over at an angle to the vertical, that of a line passing straight up from the ball and through that point at the back of your shoulders. Therefore as the club-head swings through, it comes in an arc towards the white line, passes along it at *and* just after impact, and then swings away from it again afterwards.

It is this *angled* approach to golf which makes it such an infuriatingly difficult game, and produces half the impossibly calamitous shots one sees on golf courses. There are no simple dynamics in golf at all. The actual striking forces are eternally complicated by this swing-angle.

The simplest visual impression of this angling-off of the arc is in Ben Hogan's book *The Modern Fundamentals of Golf*. He illustrates it with the idea of the club-head swinging inside a thick sheet of glass lying over the shoulders, while his head sticks through a hole in it, to look at the ball which rests in the bottom edge of the glass.

### Plane and wind-up

Your best way of appreciating this arc or plane of the swing is by addressing the ball with (say) a 5-iron and swinging back so that your whole left arm moves within this imaginary plane.

[1] It is not a circle, since your arms and club shaft are *not* in a straight line except just at and/or after impact.

Your shoulders and hips must turn like the bosses of two wheels. The swing of the left arm and club extends from the upper wheel, so that the club-head is being swung out by the centrifugal force of the wheel turning, like a weight on the end of a string. (If you don't believe this, try letting go of the club suddenly halfway up your back-swing.) The boss and spokes of this upper wheel are connected to similar points on the lower wheel round your hips by a system of elastic straps—your muscles and sinews— and the centre-shaft, your spine, is also itself elastic in torsion.

In its turn, your hip-wheel is connected to the fixed anchor-points of your feet on the ground by another complicated (and actually very powerful) elastic system of leg muscles.

NOTE: On your back-swing, the pull of the elastic drags your left hip round, and maybe your left heel off the ground; so the down-swing *begins* with a firm re-establishment of the anchor-point by swinging back the weight on to the left foot, which in turn puts a sudden extra pull on the elastic tension on the hip-wheel, which is transmitted in turn to the shoulder-wheel, and then via the *left* shoulder and arm and hand to the club and club-head.

My own feeling is that the club-head is not only at the final business end of all this unwinding in the down-swing, but it also leads the whole winding-up process in the back-swing. It cannot initiate it: you do! But you can, and I think should, initiate it by swinging back the club-head (not just the club) *as the lead-point of the winding up*. (But see pages 41, 42.)

All this really sums up the fact that *any* golf stroke is a swing, not a hit; and that the wind-up, the unwind and the follow-through are in one continuous rhythm, and very closely related to each other.

Having got it working as a swing, you also have to *groove* it into the plane. This really is important. A surprising proportion of all bad and unrewarding golf is played by those who simply haven't got the swing settled in the groove of whatever plane physically suits them.

These are the 'loopers'. You will see them everywhere; even amongst good players. But you can be fairly certain that even the odd Walker Cup looper would be a better and more consistent golfer if he could settle for a groove within the plane instead. One paramount secret of enjoying your years of golf is to swing the club-head within that plane: both up and down.

The angle of the plane to the ground must be what suits *you*. If you are short or stocky and with long arms, then it may be at a flatter angle than if you are tall and thin with short arms. And that, by the way, is the *basic* difference between what 'you will hear called respectively the flat swing and the upright swing.

Notice another essential thing, but proceeding merely from common sense and obvious mechanics. The longer the club, the flatter the swing. The shorter the club, the more upright the swing. Therefore you expect—and intend—that your swing with a driver will tend to be flatter than your swing with a chipping club.

Now, to confirm all this into the essential 'feel', take a mashie, that is (in vulgar modern terminology), a 5-iron. Hold it at the address with the left arm only, but the hand in the normal address position. Now decide to keep the left wrist rigid on this one. Not locked furiously; but simply aim *not* to allow it to bend, so that the line club-head—hand—shoulder would remain straight, as it was at the address. The wrist, in fact, *will* give slightly.

Now move it back slowly and easily to the top of the back-swing position, and then back again to the ball, all within that imaginary plane again, and rolling the whole motion around that point in your spine between your collar-bones.[1]

## How the club-face moves

Now another important thing. Most important. Essential. As you swing the club back, *allow* the club-head to turn naturally away from the ball, steadily and easily, so that when it reaches the top of the swing the *blade* of the club moves into that imaginary plane also, as the shaft reaches a horizontal position pointing towards the hole. No roll of the left wrist. Keep it as at address.

At that point, spine-pivot-point, shoulders, elbow, hand, club-shaft, heel of club, and toe of club should all lie within your chosen plane.

[1] There may be a slight variation between up- and down-swing, but don't worry about that.

On the way down, the face correspondingly closes until it returns to its original angle—square to the line of flight—of the address position through impact, and just after.

That practised, practise the follow-through from ball upwards to the finish—at which point the club-face is once again in heel-and-toe alignment (toe first this time) within the line of the imaginary plane. (In an actual stroke the swing goes on past this point through its own impetus, as you 'come up' from the ball.)

Then swing in reverse back to the address position. This swing back to the address position from the finish, though never used in an actual shot, is as much a part of the golf-swing as the three parts of it actually used in the stroke. And when you are practising swinging, don't just do the stroke, do the complete to-and-fro movement both ways. Always do this before you begin an actual game. It is the perfect formula for balance, because you can't complete this whole swing, to and fro, half a dozen times without swaying unless you *do* have everything in balance.

You just can't overestimate the usefulness of this simple practical exercise. A very useful formula for getting your game going on a Saturday morning, right from the first tee instead of only from about the 5th, *is* simply to swing your driver to and fro at least 8 times left-handed, then another 8 times right-handed; in each case in a *continuous* rhythmical series of complete swings, forward and back again, all in regular timing and rhythm.

First; it loosens you up. In the easiest and most relaxed possible way, it thus guards against strain or stiffness later; caused through bashing away from your first drive, stone cold.

No athlete in the world ever bursts from his starting blocks without having very thoroughly 'warmed up' first: and golf *is* an athletic exercise, the more so the more aggressively we 'spare ourselves no effort in order to do the ball a violent injury' (as the inimitable P. G. Wodehouse puts it, somewhere).

Second—and this can be of decisive immediate effect upon scoring—it gets the all-important hand-action into working order again; and helps at once to get the timing of your shots into the sort of operative fluency you want—and need, if you're not going to infuriate yourself with your own incompetence even more thoroughly than usual! This is true after *any* non-playing period: even of a few hours.

For the meantime, though, back to working out the mechanics and structure of your own swing: before going further.

### The left arm sets the swing

One more thing. Essential, again; and if you are a beginner you won't expect it.

It is that *the left arm controls the arc of the swing*, the arc within that plane, not just on the back- and down-swings, but also as the follow-through begins. Not the stroke, but the arc.

Think that way. The left makes the arc; it supports both the stroke itself and the after-swing of the club towards the target beyond the ball.

Certainly just as the right elbow must bend and give (elbow towards the ground, not the sky), as you swing the club back towards the top of the back-swing, so the left arm must bend and give as the right *eventually* takes over in the follow-through. But on any shot of any length it must not give until the ball is well away.

The right arm straightens as it throws its force into the impact, yes. But the left also remains straight through impact and *must* hold the arc of the swing right away from the body, against the hitting force of the right arm.

The mechanically minded will have spotted at once that this is merely the corollary of having the bottom of the swing just in front of the ball, and clipping it with the club-face as the club-face *approaches* bottom-dead-centre of the swing.

But there is more to it than that. Remember that, in chipping, I described two composite swings within the swing: the swing of the club as a whole from the shoulders, and the swing of the club-head from the hands. However hard you were to try to keep the line left shoulder—elbow—left hand—shaft—club-head straight while you swung the club back and down, *you would not succeed.* The human wrist is made to give, and will give; so that, when your arm has swung back as far as it can comfortably go, the momentum of the club-head will carry itself on, and—in effect—wind up a muscle-pull via the wrist. This always happens and is part of the good golfing swing. As the swing reverses, you are thus automatically set in the hands-ahead-of-club-head position in which you come into the ball. (If this creates no clear picture, watch a good axe-man swinging his blade; and there you have it.) The impact position is the address position plus the swinging effect.

### Wrists on the full shot

On the chip, you consciously use the hands and wrists. On the full shot, you can try to keep them straight; for they will be pulled into the power position by the momentum of the club-head. How you decide to combine these two extremes of loose, consciously directed wrist-action, and stiff-as-possible, momentum-wound wrist-action is entirely up to you. But as a beginner, if you aim (not too rigidly!) at the latter, you will probably be adopting the best practical policy. Wrist-action comes with strength and experience.

The effects of it on the swing can now be described. On the way back the momentum of the club-head will pull the wrists round sideways—thumbs towards the chin—on top of the left arm-swing from the shoulder. On the way down *do not try to reverse this sequence*. Let the left arm remain in control, and lead the swing as a whole. Swing the hands down and through, as if you were heaving on a rope (the word 'pull' helps here sometimes). The club-head will catch up, under the instinctive following-up action of the right hand, as the right arm straightens in the hit-through, and the hand itself slaps through impact: the inevitable effect of swinging the club-head on the end of the shaft.

The good player actually has swung his hands back to the line between eye and ball while the shaft of the club is still pointing above the horizontal. But don't be too ambitious at first. Don't strive directly at this position. *Swing;* and let it all happen naturally. The stronger your right hand and arm get, the harder you will be able to lead (or 'pull') down with the left arm, and the *later* will be the actual *hit* with the hands.

### The feeling of swinging, not hitting

Having at last had to bring in the word 'hit', I think the best suggestion I can make is that you should now read practically any book by Ernest Jones.

Ernest Jones has always had just one theory about golf. It is 'swing the club-head'. His book (whichever it is) will tell you to swing the club-head. As if you were swinging a pocket-knife on the end of a piece of string. (Try that. Note how the hands *have* to lead on the way down and through the ball; interesting, I think, and exactly the secret of timing.)

To return (at last; sorry we've been so far away) to the arc of the swing. Look at it again. The fact that the hands *lead* in on the way down *steepens* the arc *into* the ball. The fact that they still lead at the earliest stage of the swing-through *flattens* the arc close to the ground for two feet or so through *and after* impact (with both arms simultaneously straight in the stroke), and throws out the arc of the follow-through into a wide one, with the club-head rising from the ground much more gradually than it approaches it on the down-swing.

Don't forget to 'swing the club-head'.

And that's all there is to the basic golf-swing, although, having acquired this basic plane and arc and swing and ('swing—the—club-head')[1] timing, there are all manner of slight variations from it that you will want to try—and make use of—if the game really appeals to your intellect.

# 6

# Hitting it straight

At this point—what is the key to straightness?

It is really astonishingly simple! Two self-contained factors absolutely guarantee straightness on any shot:

[1] One of the more remarkable things about Ernest Jones is how he spends a whole book, and a whole series of books, repeating himself! But the secret of golf is a repeating swing. So why not?

1. One is that the club-head shall be swung straight through the ball towards your point of aim.
2. The other is that the club-face itself shall be pointing directly towards the same line of aim as it is swung through the ball.

1 is determined by your stance, grip, swing, and plane.

2 is determined by your holding the club-face square to the ball with your left arm and wrist and hand, during and *just after* impact. Address the ball with the club-face and left arm and wrist in the position you intend them to take at impact, and then as you swing into the ball swing them back into that position *and hold them there until the ball is away.*

It really isn't a very complicated demand on the part of the game. But if you do achieve the two simple factors above you are absolutely certain to hit a straight shot.

This is so important for future enjoyment that I'm going to leave it precisely at that.

# 7

# Enter the sweep

Still practising with your irons and pushing out the range longer and longer as you get control of them, you will come up against a consciousness of meeting something new in the game.

This is (or ought to be) a consciousness of a change in the general nature of the feel of striking the ball. This goes with the change in the general arc and angle of the plane of the swing.

As the club chosen itself gets longer, both in application and in actual length of shaft, the general arc of the swing gets wider and fuller, and the plane gets flatter. The original feeling on chip shots of the ball clipped with the fingers of the right hand has faded progressively into the feeling of it being swept away with hands, arms, body, and all. And so it is.

On a full drive there is a minimum of conscious wrist-action, the maximum of resolution to sweep the ball away with a *feeling* of straight-wristedness, and getting the body swung into the stroke behind the power of the arms. Don't forget Ernest Jones: but do let that little ball have it!

So long as your driving swing remains in balance, all *four* parts, then it's on the right lines. 'Clip' in a chip becomes 'sweep' in a drive or brassie. It's the same thing only on a larger scale and wider timing.


# 8

# Timing

**Percussion point**

Timing is two things. One, as you know, is 'swing the club-head', or 'hit late', or 'the hips then the shoulders then the arms then the hands then the shaft then the club-head, all exactly catching up with each other *just after impact*'—whichever of these three you feel the easiest way of expressing, understanding, and carrying it out! They all amount to the same thing, very much.

The other part of timing is hitting the ball with exactly the right spot on the club-face: the 'sweet spot', the Americans call it; the 'percussion point', as the scientists declare.

You know it when you feel it.

If you want to know exactly *what* it is, take a cricket bat. Hang it by a length of string (not wire) to a ceiling beam or to a branch of a tree, or to the headpiece of a doorway. Take a cricket ball, or a hammer with the face wrapped in something soft to protect the bat. Then with a swing of the arm strike the bat in the face with it.

Nearly every time the bat will twist one way or the other, or jiggle back and forward on its string. But you will eventually be able to find a precise spot on the face of the blade, a tap upon which will send the bat swinging smoothly back, with no twists, no jiggles. That spot is the percussion point, the sweet spot, the point of perfect timing—and of maximum power.

A golf club is a different sort of implement. But upon the face of a club, as upon the face of a bat, there is one point of perfect timing. You will find it by experience in play. The art of golf is to cultivate the ability always to connect with the ball in that spot. It will produce the sweetest, most accurate stroke, and the longest one for the force used.

Even a putter has one, too (very often, especially with bad designs, not at all where you expect to find it, or even where you —visually—like to address the ball on the blade). Choosing a putter that suits you is accordingly very much a question of finding one where the sweet spot is where you want it to be for the visual comfort of lining up.

### Clubs must 'feel' right

The same in general goes for all golf clubs. Choose them with care—to suit *you* by feel. Never mind what famous professional's name is or is not connected with them. You can take that—if you know your man—as a testament of good workmanship and good design (especially if he actually uses them). But you cannot take it to mean that because they suit him they will suit you.

Your home-club professional probably won't let you hit shots with a brand-new set of woods (though he may with any second-hand ones). But irons are different, especially if used from a mat. A good professional may always let you hit a few balls fairly gently, just to see how they 'feel' in your hands.

(Of course, Ernest Jones would say that so long as you swing the club-head you are bound to connect with the sweet spot and achieve perfect timing too. O.K. Try it. Anything you believe in works.)

### Rhythm

The 'Blue Danube' theory: Swing the club to and fro (all four parts of the swing) continuously in time to the 'Blue Danube Waltz' (any old-fashioned waltz will do, but that's always seemed

to me the best). Then do the same thing—*no, the same thing . . .
wait for it!*—with the ball.

This works. It can do you no conceivable harm. It may do a
lot of good. Try it, too.

# 9

# Driving

The drive is an extension of the chip. It is also an extension of
every other shot you have been reading about.

But there are two very important things about it.

One is that it has greater power to affect a man's performance
and enjoyment alike than any other stroke. The other is that it
is done with an entirely different sort of club. In an iron the face
looks at you from directly in line with the end of the shaft. With
a wooden club you are looking down the shaft at the bulge of
the club-head and the face itself is an inch or so to the left. You
are not, in fact, swinging the face of the club at the end of the
shaft. You are swinging it just in front of the end of the shaft.

Swing errors are thus automatically increased in the effect they
have. The reasons are too technical (and mathematical) to be
worth going into.

But consequently:

1. The determining factors for straightness already given are
more important than ever. You *must* swing *straight* through the
ball, and you *must* hold the club-face square to the hole, at and
through impact, if you are going to enjoy your driving.

2. The swing adopts the widest arc of which you are comfortably capable; the object is to make the part through the ball as
near a straight line parallel to the ground as possible.

3. With the brassie, spoon, and 4-wood you will find out by
practical experience when you want to sweep it away with the

flattened-base arc, and when you want to play it more like a long iron shot, i.e. taking it just before bottom dead centre.

In general, the better the lie the more you drive it: the tighter the lie the more you play it like an iron.

## 10

# Two essentials

### Knees

A tremendously potent source of bad shots, and an infallible way of making golf difficult, is playing with straight knees!

The knees should always be slightly relaxed, and never stiff. If you try to play with both legs straightened like ramrods, you kill the free-swinging movement of the hips and body, and reduce your pivoting to an incongruous discomfort that will pay full dividends only in aches and pains.

Although the swing ends on a straight left leg, the actual stroke is often made, by the very best performers, with both knees slightly bent; and certainly the knees should never be rigidly straight as the swing comes into the ball.

A neat exercise to try—if you suspect yourself of over-rigidity here—is the method which Max Faulkner always seemed to me to be using through the years around the time he won the Open in 1953. His knees seemed to dip down on the back-swing, half straighten at the top of it, then dip down again as he began to bring the stroke into the ball, to straighten again into the follow-through. The whole sequence looked to be in the most perfect of rhythm: a sort of *down*—back, *down*—through, or *um*chacha, *um*chacha effect (the second and fourth 'chas' being respectively the pause at the top during the swing's reversal of direction, and the slowing into the follow-through). Here, at any rate, is an admirable corrective exercise for the week-end golfer with the stiff-pins trouble.

**Another angle on the perfect golf shot**

Here's the balance of the game! A smooth swing of the arms, hands and clubhead: with the body revolving around that centre of gravity which holds the whole action in perfect balance.
Geoffrey Paine, leading member of the British Limbless Ex-Servicemen's Golf Society, played quite beautifully like this to a handicap of 5, when this photograph was taken. There couldn't be a much better example of what golf is all about.

Geoffrey Paine: *Barratt's Photopress*

**All golf is an extension of the chip shot**

Here is the same basic impact position – and swing-mechanics! – as for a perfect chip-shot. The back of the left wrist still swings through square towards the hole. The hands swing the clubhead after them through the ball. Then both swing together up into the follow-through.

There is so much right – indeed perfect! – about these two studies of Brian Huggett, practising iron shots, that no time spent looking at them can possibly be wasted. Here's the sure mechanical foundation of Huggett's celebrated 'gutsy' competitiveness in the very highest company on great occasions, like the ulcerous finish to the Ryder Cup Match at Birkdale in 1973.

Brian Huggett: *W. W. Neale*

**Still chipping – just extending it a bit further still!**

Another action study of a truly great player, with just about
everything right in it you could imagine. Roberto de Vicenzo
(Argentina) piling everything into that great drive of his, to delight
everybody on hand. There was no more popular champion ever
when he finally took the Open at St. Andrews in 1967, after he'd
almost given up hoping himself! (For how the golf swing takes in the
essentials shown on these 4 pages, see the sequence from page 72.)

Roberto de Vicenzo: *Frank Gardner*

### The take-away

Many professionals will tell you that the take-away of the club, the back-swing should be straight back from the ball with the club-face kept 'square'. This is good doctrine, of course. But, in the sense in which the average golfer understands it, the only man I have ever seen apparently doing it much of the time is Peter Thomson at his very best—one of the simplest and most economical of all swingers. And if the week-end golfer trains himself to take the club away facing square to the hole for too long, he tends to end by taking it back not straight but *outside* the line, and this fault leads, in its simplest forms, both to the pull-slice complex and to hitting up at the ball off the back foot and consequently sclaffing. What the pro really usually means is not rolling or shutting the club-face as it goes back.

Two old theories are eternally conflicting within this part of the swing. The first lays down that the hands should lead (ahead of the club-head) into the back-swing (which leaves the club looking towards the hole for a shade longer). About the only famous player who does this in a marked degree all the time is Locke, and with him there are remarkably good reasons, since it couples with his shut stance, vast pivot, and exaggerated in-to-out swing into the ball, to produce a reliable hook—*for him*.

If *you* seem to be sweeping the club-head away nicely on this theory, yet are still tending to snatch from the top and either pull the ball (straight) to the left, or slice it (curving) to the right, then suspect yourself of actually taking the club-head back *outside* the line.

The contrary theory is that the hands should make the club-head lead into the back-swing by thrusting it back *inside the line*, right from the moment of the forward-press before the stroke, about which the professional will have taught you. (In this method the club-face tends to turn away quickly from the line to the hole.)

This goes right back to J. H. Taylor in his original book with Beldam (and no doubt a long way beyond that). The most instructive thing about it is that, if you begin the back-swing by sweeping the club-head back with the arms and wrists from the forward position, you have only to carry the same movement straight round until the club points to the hole at the top of the back-swing to be in a good position. This is sometimes advised by teachers to correct an out-to-in trouble.

I suspect that for the *average* golfer, and for many (but not all) developing good ones, this may be the wisest way to start the swing, particularly since it also seems to encourage a late hit, a balanced swing-through, and good timing and balance. It feels simpler, too, and is more closely related to the basic hand-action in the short shots, especially chipping, than the other method.

The drag-away, hands leading, on the other hand, can produce extremely long and/or powerful shots. Against it is its tendency to lead to looping—for an extreme example of which see any old action-pictures of James Bruen: a genius entirely on his own.

The best wisdom I know on this whole point is the summing-up—a most deceptively simple one for the amount of vital truth there is in it—by Henry Cotton in his book *This Game of Golf*[1] (page 57):

'Unfortunately all golf is a question of regular compensation; there is no finality, and once a player has acquired a good action, these little points, say at the beginning of the back-swing, change the timing and often the whole action. Now I can think for a period of beginning hands-first myself, and get a beautiful rhythm which I can keep for a long time, but to say I always think of that as the initial movement is untrue, as I get to the point of exaggerating this finally, as everybody does, and then I go to the opposite extreme, which is club-head first, to restore a balance.'

The operative words here are '*as everybody does*'. Sweep the club away hands first, club-head low, and you will sooner or later need to give yourself a dose of the club-head-back-inside-first corrective and, probably, vice versa.

[1] *Country Life* (1948).

# II

# Style and method: a few check-points

*First Aid*

Throughout this book, I am assuming that the beginner, or anyone else who wants really to get to grips with the game, would acquire his basic method from the professional. But we can't all be running to and from the professional all the time; and things go wrong in course of play of the most basic and fatal character.

So the purpose of this chapter is to go over some of the things most likely to go wrong during a game—or indeed at any time: a sort of series of mental check-points against which the player can measure himself.

They are all ones which my own sufferings, both as a player and as a professional watcher, make me believe are vital. Some men can ignore them, and still play well. But most will find things go very much more easily if they stick to them.

### The hands
Whatever grip the professional originally taught you, you will tend periodically to depart from it.

The Vs between thumbs and forefingers are two essential check-points. They can both point anywhere between the right shoulder and the chin, and still be perfectly correct. That much latitude the mechanics of the game allow. But anything outside that should be looked upon with the deepest of suspicion.

There may indeed be a particular odd exception in the case of the left hand; for there are players—and good players—who produce their best results with the V between the *left* thumb and forefinger pointing to the *left* of the chin.

Hardly any man, though, ever played his potentially best

golf with the V of the *right* hand pointing outside the *right* shoulder. And this is a fault you will observe in numbers of handicap players who make your friends at week-ends. It is a foolishness, for it turns the swing very much into a hit in most cases; and at best it means that the player has got to do some other odd things to compensate for it.

As a guide: If you are slicing, check that your hands (or one or the other of them) are not outside the limits, to the left. If you are pulling, check that neither is outside the limits to the right.

The characteristics of the two extremes *within* these limits are roughly as follows:

*Hands to extreme right*, i.e. both Vs pointing at right shoulder: Power, especially for recovering from rough and for long driving; tendency to hit instead of swing encouraged. Makes it easier to play a hook—intentionally or unintentionally. Tendency to lead the ordinary player to hold his hands too far back at the address, and to get the club-head ahead of the hands into or through impact (which can cause either a quick hook or a slice or all manner of other things. See page 85!) Can encourage any tendency to hit up at the ball, particularly on chip shots.

*Hands to extreme left*, i.e. both Vs pointing at the chin: Less power and less length of drive for the ordinary player (though Ben Hogan at one time gripped like this and played superlatively). Tendency to cause a slice through weakness of hands not getting the club-head crisply through; but—correspondingly—it can make a good grip for the intentional low fade. Good for hooded-faced chips and pitches. Can (in theory but hardly ever in practice) lead the ordinary player to have his hands too far ahead of the ball at the address; few ordinary players are in fact ever likely to have their hands too far ahead of the ball at impact in the true sense of the phrase, though this grip (as said above) can tend to slow up the hand-action to such an extent that the club-head comes in still slightly open, and probably across the ball from out-to-in.

*Ideal combination at address for many good players:* Left-hand V pointing to chin, right-hand V pointing between chin and right shoulder.

*Ideal combination for many less-strong players:* Left-hand V pointing just to the right of the chin, right-hand V pointing just inside the right shoulder.

NOTE: *Knuckle-business:* You will come across talk of 'showing how many knuckles' of the left hand. As you can easily see, left-hand V aimed at chin gives you a 'one-knuckle' grip; left V aimed at right shoulder gives you a 'three-knuckle' grip. But individual variations of hand make-up and suppleness come in here. A good general rule (which corresponds with what is said above) is: when meaning to keep the ball low, grip showing one knuckle; when meaning to send it high, grip showing three knuckles. But this again is for individual experiment; and works exactly the opposite way for some people. (Who'd be a professional!)

### Right hand

The professional will have taught you at some time to hold the club in the fingers and palm combined of the left hand, in the *fingers only* of the right.

One of the commonest faults of really bad golfers is to grip the club in the *palm* of the right hand. It is comparatively easy for the beginner, or the improving player, to slip back into this. This is the *hitting* position, not the *swinging*. Eschew it emphatically, and at all times: except perhaps very occasionally in the most desperately thick of rough. There is probably no grip fault in the whole game which has more disastrous effect upon touch, feel, and sensitivity than this one.

The club must be *swung*, in the left hand, with the *fingers* of the right hand providing timing, accuracy, strength, and blade-control generally. The left thus becomes the *firm*, almost the static, hinge of the hand-action, the right wrist the fluent and moving one.

### Left arm

The modern fashion is against a rigidly straight left arm. Far more players, though, commit faults through bending the left arm than through holding it too rigid. Check that it is not getting sloppy—*particularly through impact*. Collapse of the left arm at the elbow, as the club comes into the ball, is a potent cause of quick-hooking, and of impotent shots generally.

The left wrist is the pivot-point of the hand-action; it is essential to swing out the whole arm authoritatively from the left shoulder to guide the total swing firmly through the most effective arc (see chapter on iron play).

### Right elbow

It is a fact that golf was once played very cheerfully by men in jackets with the right elbow flourishing high in the air on the back-swing. But they were playing with a different type of ball and a larger and more whippy type of club with plenty of twist in the shaft; no professional would recommend the flying right elbow as helpful today.

There is a well-known American professional who suggests that you think of it as 'The Waiter's Elbow'; and have it at the top of the swing in the forearm-vertical position of a waiter carrying a tray of drinks on a spreadeagled right hand. This may be going just a bit too far—it depends on your joints; but most players are far more likely to err in the other direction, of allowing the elbow to float out towards the horizontal.

### Left wrist-action

Either you cock or you don't.[1] If the left wrist is flat at the top of the swing, or even bulbed slightly outwards, then you are not cocking (and probably swinging flat as well). If it is cocked back, so that the knuckles would be visible to an eye behind your left elbow, then it is in the 'cocked' position.

Many of the most famous golfers in the world have played with that cocked position. But for the beginner, and the week-end golfer (particularly, for some reason, the ladies amongst them), any over-generously cocked *left* wrist often leads to a flat *right* wrist, or a floating right elbow, or both!

Try experimenting with three positions:

1. Back of left wrist flat at top, right wrist cocked (club-face shut).

2. Back of right wrist flat at top, left wrist cocked (club-face open).

[1] This section is simplified—see note on cocking, at end of chapter.

3. Positions in between. Here is the compromise area where you will probably find your golfing home.

### Club-face at top

Following on from that choice of cocking, or not cocking, the left wrist, and intimately tied up with it, is the matter of club-face 'open', 'shut', or 'square' at the top.

'Square' is the middle (and on the whole to be recommended) position. It is so called because if you take your club in your left arm only, square it to the ball, and then swing back without turning your left wrist either way, this is the position the club-face will reach at the top. It will be facing neither the sky nor the horizon, but halfway between the two, and the blade will lie within the plane of the swing.

'Shut' is the position easily reached by taking the club back with a flattish swing and a completely flat left wrist. At the top of the swing, the *toe* of the club-head is pointing to the right of the target, with the blade facing the sky and almost parallel with the left arm, while the club-shaft itself is pointing to the *left* of the target.

This is the low-hitting hooker's position, often also used by good players fading the ball intentionally. As that mere sentence expresses it, it is a method where two simultaneous off-line points of technique are used in a marriage producing—it is hoped—straight progeny! It has the vitality of a marriage between dissimilars—and many of the storms; I think it puts a bit more strain on the spine than the other methods.[1]

'Open' is the position reached by an extreme backward cock of the left wrist, and very little cock of the right, coupled very often with a backward roll of the club-head at the top of the swing. The *toe* of the club then points down towards the ground, almost parallel with the line of the right forearm, with the blade facing the horizon opposite you, while the shaft as a whole points to the right of the target.[1]

---

[1] A flat swing, with a flat left wrist, can be made open at the top by a clockwise roll of the wrists. Similarly an upright swing can be shut at the top by an anti-clockwise roll of the wrists. Neither to be recommended!

This position can be used for hitting the ball perfectly straight and easily, if coupled with the rolling movement of the wrists. It is probably the easiest and least straining of all methods of hitting a golf ball; with the modern small, hard, heavy ball, and the modern heavy, stiff-shafted clubs. Play this way and you'll last for ever, but—unless you are naturally a very good player—you'll hit a lot of crooked shots.

In golf, as in most things, the mean method suits the majority of people most of the time. But, as in most other things, any individual may prove an exception to the general rule.

Perhaps the best thing for any man to do—especially as he begins to master the easier parts of the game—is to teach himself to be able to use all three methods, depending on what is needed.

Obviously, his ordinary 'repeating' swing must be built round one chosen position. But the shut-faced swing to push the ball low into a wind can be tremendously useful—especially with a 2-iron off a windy tee; and the open-faced position can be very useful, not only for producing a cut-up shot, and short pitches, but for raising the ball high in the air at any stroke.

We could add, here, one interesting and probably significant phenomenon, which is not completely easy to explain. With a shut face the ball can be pushed, forced, hit, or swung away. With an open face the ball *must* be swung away, and swung only. I don't quite know why this is. But it is a fact.

### Hands in impact
Are you still sure your hands are coming into the stroke first, and are level with the ball before the club-head has come in?

### Feet
One or two of the most efficient professionals address the ball not only with a closed stance but also with their toes (particularly the right) pointing back, *beyond* a right angle to the direction of aim. If they can do it, you can, if you like. But I think the whole question of stance was best summed up by Ben Hogan in his book (which incidentally echoed Harry Vardon's of sixty years earlier). Right foot at right angles to the line to the target; left foot slightly open, if anything, i.e. at slightly less than a right angle to the line to target.

If things are going wrong, then, try checking that your right foot has not crept round to point away from the target. One sees bad golfers in thousands trying to play with the right foot in this position and making things difficult for themselves: difficult because from this position it is all the easier to stay back on the right foot during the stroke; and all the harder to swing the weight properly through towards the hole.

This is just about the most important thing, incidentally, for most week-end golfers; *getting out of your own way*, so as to be able to swing freely straight-onwards right through the shot, and up into the follow-through.

Few things, for most people, make more certainly for bad golf than trying to swing against, around, or across (as many spare-time golfers too often do) the sort of shut stance from which only a supple athlete can really play consistent golf.

What matters decisively, in any shot, is far more how directly your body-shoulder-and-arms-swing is aligned towards your target, than upon how your feet are set. The feet alignment serves only to place any golfer in the most comfortable, powerful, easily-controlled, and easy-working position (for him or her) from which body weight and body muscles, working together, can generate power; and discharge it outwards into the swinging of the club-head through the ball, straight on target.

The norm remains always this: if you are 'bending them', try standing square, i.e. with the line from right toe to left toe pointing at the target. You may prefer—out of habit—to stand open or closed; but, *if* you are bending them, *try* standing square.

### Weight

The weight should be firmly moving on to the left leg at impact (or rather just before it), and should stay there until the end of the stroke. The follow-through to a full shot should thus end in perfect balance on the left leg, with the right foot and leg *relaxed* and the heel pulled naturally partly off the ground. The weight moves with the swing, generating momentum, and timing.

If you have any doubts about whether you are doing this, check it carefully on a practice swing. (*See illustration: page 65.*)

If you are falling back, and hitting the ball off the right leg, then *you will already* be leading yourself into all manner of troubles and difficulties: noticeably slicing, topping, sclaffing, quick-hooking, and giving up golf!

The hands and the weight move through ahead of the ball together (least on a sweeping drive, most on a delicate little chip) to provide the momentum and balance of the shot, superimposed upon which the hand-action brings the club-head roaring in, through, straight for the target, and up to the finish of the swing.

### Rhythm

The surest thing I know to prove or disprove the rhythm of your swing is to address an imaginary ball and then swing continuously backwards and forwards through it, without changing or adjusting grip, stance, or anything. If you can do this without overbalancing or swaying about, then your rhythm and your balance are just about right—on the practice swing, anyway. Reproduce the same rhythm in actual shots—and the basis of balance and timing is laid.

A useful practice-ground trick to help inculcate this is to line up twenty balls at right angles to the direction you intend to hit them, each about four or five inches apart; then begin with the first and, with a steady continuous to-and-fro swing, send them all off one after another, moving the right foot a shade forward as you begin each reverse follow-through, and the left foot up to it as you begin each down-swing.

When you can hit all twenty perfectly accurately and without strain, and without any pause in the *regular* rhythm of the swing, then you have the hang of balance. Never mind if anyone thinks you have taken leave of your senses, or are simply trying tc show off. That is the essential rhythm of golf. The old-fashioned waltz rhythm is ideal for this twenty-ball balance-and-timing exercise.

### Eye

Well, *are* you looking at it? And did your eye spot the divot mark made by the shot, before you began to look up after the ball?

**Top of back-swing—further check**

1. Are you comfortably balanced, with the weight rather more on the right foot than the left?

2. Have you pivoted freely, or is your club-shaft pointing at the top markedly to the *left* of the target?

If it is, do you really mean to play a hooded-faced fade? Or are you, on the contrary, really trying to play golf the simple way? If the latter, then you are in a wrong position—unless you habitually swing with a flat left wrist.

3. If you play with a fully cocked left wrist, are you by any chance overdoing it?

The prime symptom of overdoing it is the floating right elbow: it is 'floating' if your right forearm is not more or less close to the vertical at the top of the back-swing. If you are using a *fully* cocked *left* wrist, your *right* wrist should be *flat* at the back, or almost so.

*For most people, the easiest position to hit the ball from is one in which the backs of both wrists are very slightly creased at the top—by just the about same amount.*

**Note on cocking**

In the above chapter, striving after clarity, I have deliberately simplified beyond the bounds of strict truth, here and there.

'Cocking' in golf is by usage taken to mean this: Clench your hands in front of you with the wrists straight and the forearms horizontal. Now, without moving your forearms, turn your hands upwards towards your eyes until you can just see the tips of the knuckles of the little fingers. That is 'cocking' the wrists. Drop them back to the straight-wristed angle, and that is 'uncocking'.

To see it even more simply: take a hammer, keep the forearm horizontal, and, using the wrist only, swing the hammer as if you were driving a nail vertically downwards into the top of a table. Cocking the wrist lifts the hammer. Uncocking it makes the stroke to drive the nail in. This is exactly what is happening with the wrists in golf—or ought to be.

Now take the hammer in both hands. Cock the wrists together and drive the nail in, with the hammer straight in front of you: the simplest action, and basic to the golf stroke.

Now turn your wrists so that the shaft of the hammer makes a straight line with the *left* wrist and forearm up to the elbow. To do this you have to bend back your right wrist, crinkling it deep at the back. There you have your 'flat-left-wrist-at-the-top' position.

Turn them the other way, hammer-shaft in line with right wrist to right elbow, and there you have your 'maximum-left-wrist-cock-at-the-top' position.

At the moment of impact you can have the left wrist still slightly cocked back (for a high shot or an intentional high hook) or you can hold it (or even move it) straight and square into impact, rather like a back-hand drive in tennis. Even the weekend golfer of no great ambitions can use this. If you are terrified of hooking your wife into those gorse bushes, when all square at the 18th in the club mixed foursomes, then square your left wrist through impact and (other things being equal) you won't hook!

Another way of putting this is: 'Play the shot back-hand with the *left forearm and wrist ahead of the club-head.*'

## 12

# Methods of getting out of trouble

It is commonly believed amongst club golfers that the basis of real recovery play is strength.

That is true so far as it goes, obviously. But it is not the whole truth. Strength alone is not enough—as many a man of mighty muscle proves and re-proves every week-end!

I am not particularly strong myself. In fact the average Ryder Cup professional could sew me up with one hand held behind his back. But if it came to a straight contest between him and me, at getting balls out of thick or rough gorse bushes, then the contest would be very much closer—mostly because I have, willy-nilly, spent a far greater part of my golfing life doing this sort of thing than he has!

Recovery play stands about equally upon:

1. Strength of hands and wrists, coupled with technique.
2. An intelligent *mechanical* assessment of the proposition.
3. A weighing-up of the best balance of risk against possible reward.
4. Optimism, courage, boldness, foolhardiness, or sheer tomfoolery—whichever you prefer to call it.

1. Even though strength is largely a matter of natural physique and experience, let no one run away with the idea that recovery players are born and not made. Practically everyone—including a woman—has enough strength to make a first-class recovery player—so long as the strength is trained by practice and is *practically* applied.

It is no good at all just thrashing all-out at the rubbish surrounding the ball, in the rough direction of the ball itself. It works sometimes. But more often it doesn't. The secret (nearly always, but not always) is to play the shot with a nicely judged action of the wrists.

Sometimes you want to use nearly all wrist. Sometimes you want to use a great sweep of the left arm, with the right more or less forcing the club-head through and up. Sometimes you want to chop, or hack, or even balloon it out. But what these choices all have in common is that the shot must be *timed*. One can say, without any real abuse of the meaning of the words, *that even a hack must be a swing*! And that every single ordinary recovery shot must have an *acceleration into the follow-through*—even if the follow-through never actually materializes, through obstruction of the club-head by vegetable of various kinds and consistencies!

In sheer technique, though, one factor is nearly always a *sine qua non*: the left arm and hand. However much hand-action or slash you are going to use, the pivot of the hand-action can only be in that butt of the left hand. Unless that is supported resolutely by the firmest of swings of that left arm through the ball, then everything is likely to collapse. It is (nearly always) no good doing everything right with the stroke-making right hand, if the whole attempt founders on an insecure fulcrum.

In actual execution, the aim is:

(a) Swing the club-face accurately through the ball in perfect timing.

(b) Swing to follow-through with utmost freedom—even if you know the follow-through is going to be stopped.

(c) *When appropriate*, follow through to swing the cutting edge of the club sharply upwards *immediately after* the ball is hit.

This is partly the corollary of holding the club short (even, if you need to, down on to the metal part of the shaft) and using maximum hand-swing.

(d) Often, in the thickest of trouble, a pronounced in-to-out rolling action of the hands, taking the ball toe first and then throwing out the toe of the club towards your line of aim, will prove the safest way of *being absolutely certain* of extracting the ball to a suitably playable position (if possible, a holeable one: why not?).

2. The mechanical assessment of the position is strictly one of fact, depending on the answers to the following check-points (which, of course, you soon come to assess automatically without thinking specifically about each one in turn):

Is anything going to impede the club-face during the last six inches or so into the ball? If so, can I swing the club-head straight through that six-inch approach? If the answer to that is 'No', then which of the four alternative methods is possible, and/or looks most certain to bring the club-face into the ball: The out-to-in open-faced cut? The in-to-out toe-first hook? The under-the-obstacle arm-sweep? The over-the-obstacle hands-chop?

If all look pretty dubious: 'Can I get it out right, or left, or even back towards the tee? If there's an alternative here, which looks likely to give the most promising next shot?'

Now examine the problem of the tactics of the placing of the shot. Does it need a stiff-wristed sweep for maximum safety of extraction, or does it call for hand-action for delicacy? What's going to happen on the follow-through?

Has the ball itself got to be driven through tripe on its way up and out; and, if so, how much extra force must be given it to allow for this? (A similar problem to starting a long putt through a patch of thick grass.) Has the club-edge got to cut through anything on its way to the ball (a bramble-stalk, a bracken-stalk, a side-shoot of a bush, a pile of leaves, a tuft of grass, or turf, or peat) and if so, again, how much extra force is called for in the swing to preserve acceleration into the ball?

Sometimes, as for instance when a thick tuft or root lies behind the ball, it may be necessary to chop down on what would otherwise ideally have been played high. Concentrate then on propelling the ball forward, and make some calculation of how it may bounce over any further obstacle.

Sometimes it may even be safer to attempt a dangerous-looking shot between trees or bushes further up, but *from a simple angle of the lie*, than to attempt to hit it straight out on the fairway sideways *from an awkward angle to the lie*. The more resolute shot often pays off.

3. The balance of risk speaks for itself. But never calculate purely the penalties of failure; always look at the possible comparative reward of playing successfully bold or playing successfully safe.

4. Courage! If you hit it squarely as you mean to, it *must* come out. Moreover, it must end up more or less where you want it to. The ball has absolutely no choice in the matter! It's all entirely determined by that split-second in which the club-face connects with it.

An old rule, there, I think, applies. When having a go, relax and let rip enthusiastically! When playing safe, concentrate and be careful!

### A few notes on tough lies of particular characteristics

*Roots, brambles, thick young gorse, etc.:* Watch the ball like anything, and be extra firm with it. Only the *swing* of the cutting edge will get through these.

*Green bracken:* The ball will fly out through bracken, but the club-head will not easily swing down through it: the ball *bursts* out, the club *collects* its own opposition. Calculate accordingly.

*Dead bracken in winter:* A spoon will go through it, even the stalks. The thing to be careful of is that the club-face hits the ball in its centre, and doesn't sclaff under it.

*Stony lies, beaches, etc.:* If you can take the ball cleanly, and the club-face picks it up neatly, then almost an ordinary shot is possible. But a bit of cut-up helps, though clear of the ground. Watch it, though: even if your clubs are insured, it's a pity to break them—and flying stone-chips can be unpleasant.

*Bare sandy lies:* If you can take the ball cleanly, then you can play any shot your normal skill would enable you to play clean-hit from a close-mown fairway. But if you touch the sand behind the ball, the shot will foozle. (Except with a spoon, whose round bottom can enable it to skate or ride over the last inch or so into the ball without catastrophe, which can enable you to take wood out of a sandy lie even when the ball is not standing up too well. Push the hands back a bit this time, though; you've got to ride over the sand on the *trailing* edge of the bottom of the club-head: the general cut-up stance and swing obviously suit this situation.)

*Bracken mould, old grass cuttings, leaves:* The obvious danger here is to dig under the ball and sky it. The club-head will force its way through them on its path to the ball (with varying freedom depending on consistency and wetness); but the result will be a fluff or a skied shot unless you bring the middle of the club-face slap against the ball. Occasionally, though, particularly on short pitches on to a green, you can most safely *balloon* the ball out, with a stroke closely akin to that used in light dry sand. This can only be a safety-first shot, of course; never a delicate one to be stiff.

*Mud and plugged lies:* This can only be real hack-work! Decide precisely how much of the earth's surface you want to remove with the ball, visualize it *in toto* as your target, and then go at it. (The lump, strip, or chunk should preferably include the ball.)

*Balls embedded in steep surfaces:* Here things are not so difficult as they look. Unless this is the side of a stream, pond, or cliff, gravity is on your side—a quite infallible ally. So long as —by hitting hard into the retaining material within an inch of the ball, with a blow aimed to pass somewhere *behind* the ball—you can dislodge it from its bed, gravity will do the rest, and bring it

**Two who've holed 1000 five-footers!**

**Bob Charles**: tall, lanky, calm, New Zealander. (Prides himself on being 'British'! and don't forget it!) Probably the best putter in the world since Bobby Locke. Achieved the palpably impossible at the Royal Lytham and St. Annes Open in 1963. Left with a putt of 12 feet, to tie, after his young American opponent had holed a longer one then danced a jig and slammed his hat over the hole, Charles twitched not a muscle in his face, then calmly stroked his straight in. There never was a more impossible putt; nor a more impeccable one. (Nor golfer, ever!) 'Charger' **Arnold Palmer,** richest player of all: on putts that dropped, and dropped – and dropped! (Nowadays, he's not *quite* so sure of them. No-one is, in the end.)

Bob Charles: *Peter Dazeley*/Arnold Palmer: *Syndication International*

**Putting: A study in hands and styles**

Bob Charles again, on a longer putt. Feet further apart for the longer stroke – but blade still going through low, square towards the hole. What a comfortable, compact, easy, but highly-controlled method his is!

Bob Charles: *H. W. Neale*

Tom Weiskopf (above) and Peter Oosterhuis (right) underline lessons from Charles' method. Compact, simple, smooth, blade-towards-hole after impact. Note that all six of the highly successful players shown on these four pages of action studies use a reverse overflap putting-grip, first finger of left hand spread outside fingers of right.

The millions of week-end golfers who don't do this, of course, must know better! (Say that again?)

Tom Weiskopf: *Peter Dazeley*/Peter Oosterhuis: *E. D. Lacey*

**A man who can putt like a magician – or like the rest of us!**

When the magic is with him Tony Jacklin can steam them in from all over the place; and 8 footers drop of routine. When it goes, he can be human almost down to common level: the stroke stays masterly, but the hole moves!

Here, anyway, are again all points of a Championship putting method. (And if Charles never looks as worried as that, that's just Charles: unique!)

Tony Jacklin: *E. D. Lacey*

down into an unembedded lie. (Be careful it doesn't hit your legs, though.) Whether you choose to play the stroke vertically downwards, sideways, or bravely upwards (in the hope of extracting the ball on to altogether better ground) will vary with the circumstances. The downward blow is sometimes safest, but will contrarily sometimes drive the ball even further in (since the stroke and gravity are working in the same direction) if miss-hit.

Whichever way, hands always *well* in front of the ball: if you merely catch it on its nose with the edge of the sole of the club, the odds are you'll drive it into a new and more frightful bed. (Use a sharp-edged niblick, naturally.)

## Summary

In no shot in golf is the fundamental rule of the game more absolutely essential: *look at the ball until you've hit it*. At no time is the temptation to look up to watch it fly up and out more strong; and on no stroke is it likely to be quite so fatal. Look up and you'll leave it there. Apply yourself to the ball—and the ball will do the rest.

There is one other (and repeatable) fundamental in recovery shots of a tougher nature—in fact in all recovery shots. The thing will come off on one condition only, with complete certainty—and that is *if the club-face swings through the ball*. This sounds so elementary as to be almost absurd. But it is a fact that more recovery shots are foozled through the club-head simply not hitting the ball.

Look closely to see whether things are soft beneath it, or hard. One of the simplest fluffs of all is that which comes through overestimating the difficulty of the shot, and cutting through right underneath it without striking the ball itself properly at all.

*Final irritating note on recovery play:* No one ever recovered from anywhere on a perfectly judged back-swing. It's the forward stroke into the follow-through that does it.

# 13

# The technique of putting

Putting you can be a master of from the start. Putting is a good
eye, a good sense for the run of the ball, and the simple confidence
that you are going to make the ball do what you want it to.
There is no department of the game—or probably of any game—
in which world-class players, the absolute beginner, and the
club handicap player are on such equal terms.

No complicated technique whatsoever is needed to knock a
ball six feet into a hole in the ground $4\frac{1}{4}''$ in diameter. Even in
the exciting and nerve-tensing conditions of a close match, a
monthly medal (or the Open Championship), it must always be
a matter of a clear eye, courage, ability to rise above the quavers,
and sheer personal individual determination.

There are three sides to putting: tactics, technique, and the
particular considerations of putting 'under pressure'.

Since we have already had something of a welter of technique
in this book, let's take the tactics first. They have in them, also,
in the simplest form, the germ of all tactics in the game.

Let's assume that you have put your iron shot on to the green,
but quite a long way from the hole—between ten and fifteen
yards. What counts next?

### Putting's commonsense tactics

Your first object is to lay the long putt so close to the hole
that you cannot miss the next. In doing this, the length of the
putt will count for much more than the exact line. This is a
lesson that many golfers never really assimilate into their game
—however aware they are of the truth of it. It is comparatively
easy—except on unusual ground—to hit the putt straight enough
to pass the hole within eighteen inches on either side—and that

is close enough for holing out. But what is difficult is to get the ball to stop rolling exactly as it comes past the hole within that three-foot bracket of line on either side, and stay within the eighteen-inch radius circle of 'unmissability'.

You cannot do this by calculating strength as you hit the ball. It is like other shots in golf; the information from the eye must go into the brain and translate itself into feel for the shot—a sort of individual automatic reaction. What you can do, though— and must do—is to make sure that you have done all you can to feed into your brain the most accurate information.

When you see a great player in some tournament or championship walking up and down the line of the putt, apparently looking for earwigs, or wandering off to one side as if to see if it would make a good subject for a water-colour, or going beyond it as if to reassure himself that the hole still looks round from that side too, consciously, or (much more probably) unconsciously, he is answering a number of questions for himself and letting the information feed into his brain.

## 1. Looking along the line

How thick is the grass, how smooth is the surface, are there any irregularities which might speed up or obstruct the ball in its passage? Are the grass blades tending to lie all one way or the other (known as a 'nap' and very common nowadays when greens are kept longer than they used to be)—which will tend to speed up the ball *in* the direction the blades are lying, slow it down *against* the direction they are lying, or to help turn it away sideways *towards* the direction they are lying.

Are there irregularities nearer the hole, where they will affect the ball quite strongly as it is slowing down, or further away from the hole where they will affect it less, since it is travelling faster with more effective momentum?

An example or two:

(a) He sees the grass is bare and smooth all the way up till about six feet short of the hole, and then becomes thick and green to a point some way past it. Decision: roll the ball firmly across the smooth bit, knowing that it will be bound to be slowed up on the thicker patch around the hole—a bold putt.

The danger here is that a putt jollied over the smooth bit would die too quickly on the tough bit.

(*b*) He sees that the grass is thick, and napped against him most of the way to the hole, but that the last third of its distance is over smooth, worn grass, over which the ball will run fast. Aim: to give it just enough strength to get through the slower patch, and then coast on slowly towards the hole—a cautious putt. The danger here is much more likely to be to come through the thick patch with too much speed still on the ball, so that it careers past the hole and leaves a very nasty four-foot putt over the smooth, fast surface.

In the first of these cases his attention will be on the strength needed *over the last two or three yards*; on the second that needed *over the first seven.*

## 2. Looking at it from the side

Is the roll up or down hill to the hole? Decision: if it is uphill, then the difference in travel between one hit just too hard and one hit just too gently will not be a great deal. So it is best policy to be bold, and aim to be past the hole. (Exception: with two putts for the championship, a player might aim to be short with his first putt, to leave himself a little uphill putt to hole, which he will be able to afford to hit boldly.)

If the putt is downhill, then small errors in strength will have a greater effect than usual on distance travelled, and somehow (and possibly illogically) the danger will be to go too far past the hole in the first putt. Decision: to make sure of not being dangerously past the hole with the putt—to jolly it down the hill and let it die slowly towards the hole.

If he sees that his putt is uphill over the first part, then levels out towards the hole, his reaction is likely to be similar to the case where the grass is thick at first, and faster near the hole— i.e. aim to get it over the crest of the upslope at the right strength to carry on to the hole. If he sees the putt is flat or downhill to begin with, then uphill to the hole, the aim must be much more to give it the right firm strength to run up the final hill to the hole.

## Looking from behind the ball and behind the hole

This is done to sort out the 'borrows'. A borrow is a sideways slope along the putt, which will make it turn off one way or the other. Considerations applying:

1. A sideways borrow *early on* in the putt will affect it far less than a late one, since the ball's momentum will carry it over the borrow with little turning off from the line upon which it was struck.

2. A borrow coming up to the hole must be treated with more care, particularly on fast greens or where the part around the hole is worn smooth with use. Since the ball will run into this slope when its momentum is dying, and it is travelling slowly, then most likely it will be considerably affected by the sideways pull of the borrow. Further, if it is still on the 'up' side of the hole as it approaches it, it will turn in towards the hole as it eases to rest and will tend to end up near it. If it has already passed from the 'up' to the 'down' side of the borrow as it nears the hole, then *each extra turn will be taking it away from the hole*, and a bit too much run will leave a nasty longish one to hole.

There is a good reason indeed for the latter type of ball being called ending on 'the amateur side', the former on 'the professional side'.

Remember too—as experience emphatically teaches—that a sideways borrow on an uphill putt, or on longish grass (or both), will have much more effect on the ball, particularly near the hole, than the same borrow on the downhill putt, or a putt over a smooth fast surface.

As a general rule, wherever the ball is going to come in to the hole on a sideways borrow, it is usually safest to aim well on the professional side, and be sure not to be too strong with it; a ball dying just short as it turns in towards the hole on a borrow is likely to leave a much shorter second putt than a ball running over-boldly past it. If you want to play your holing-out putt from beyond the hole, then give it the extra boldness but aim to run past the hole even more safely on the 'up' side, i.e. 'borrow' a bit extra on your line of aim.

Above all there are two rules:

(*a*) Where there is a borrow, aim to come to rest on the 'professional side', the 'up' side of the hole, on any long putt.

(*b*) The *strength* of the putt, on whatever line you hit it, is what decisively determines whether the next putt will be a knock-in or a nasty one.

(All the above rules, of course, also apply to chipping and, to a lesser extent, to pitching, though in the latter case the aim may be not so much to lay the ball stiff by the hole as to make sure of laying it in a position from which it is easy to lay the first putt stone dead. The tactics of the pitch are the tactics of the putt—but on a slightly larger scale, taking in the shape and contours and surface of the green as a whole. You should never be in any danger of taking three putts after a pitch of anything up to seventy-five yards. Nor is there any reason why you should be. When practising, this is the most important part of the tactics of the pitch shot to concentrate on; and thus *line* may sometimes be more important than length, especially across the wind.)

### Tactics of short putts

There are two ways of holing a short putt. One is to concentrate on giving it exactly the right strength to reach a point about six inches past the hole; so that, if it touches the hole anywhere, it will do so as a 'dying ball' and will drop in. The other is to concentrate on hitting it firmly straight at the back of the hole.

*Dying ball:* Advantages: you cannot possibly miss the next! Disadvantages: ball more easily deflected from its course by small irregularities of surface, or by slight borrow, than when it is hit harder. The more borrow exists, then the more you should aim to enter the hole from the 'up' side of the borrow. *When to use:* fast downhill putts.

*Hit the back of the hole:* Advantages: slightly more easy to hit the ball on the line you intend. Ball unlikely to be so much affected by surface irregularitites or even by borrow. Disadvantages: danger of running past the hole, and missing the next one.

When using this method, never overestimate the effect of borrow. A ball hitting anything but the middle of the back of he hole may, if travelling firmly, hit the inside of the rim, but twist out again by the force of its own momentum. *When to use:* slow or uphill putts, or over a rough surface.

(NOTE, THOUGH: In match-play, or bogey-play, when the first putt must go down for a half, there is obviously a corresponding premium on the bold, authoritative putt—since the next one will not have to be played anyway.)

This is by no means all there is to putting tactics. But any player working on the above lines will inevitably pick up the nuances for himself. Those who never really think their putts out, remain all their lives entirely unreliable putters. But so do those whose hands just will not obey their brains—a matter of technique.

### Putting methods

Here we enter a realm of cloud cuckoo-land! Just as ordinary handicap golfers often putt remarkably well with outlandishly unorthodox styles and methods, so some of the best putters in the world advocate—and often use—methods in direct contradiction of each other, both in theory and in mechanics.

It is a field in which any golfer at all is perfectly justified in using any method that appeals to him, so long as it works in practice. Of course, those who play golf for the sheer fun of it, and never have to face the problems of putting under the tremendous nervous tension of championship conditions, have very much more latitude in their choice of methods, and the free-and-easiness of their whole approach.

Here, more for interest and experiment than for example, are some of the most clear-cut methods used successfully by good players:

*The free-swinging, traditional, or caddie-boy method.* Stand square, feet close together, and swing the putter straight back and forth almost entirely from the hands. This is the swing, and 'touch', method *par excellence*; and it is particularly effective on longer putts where the strength of the stroke, the feel for it, matters more than anything. It is also the simplest and most relaxed of all methods. The length of back-swing equals the length of fore-swing, and the ball is just sent sweetly away as the putter is swung in the hands.

It all relies on natural *swinging* instinct, and thus has a closer affinity, perhaps, with the rest of the game than any other putting method.

*The pendulum method.* In this there is the same reliance on swinging. But the swing is used from the shoulders instead of from the hands. The wrists are kept straight and firm, and the club is swung in one piece with the arms. The result is a low, flat sweep through the ball, and perhaps less liability to turn the blade off the line as the ball is struck.

NOTE the close parallel here in these two methods with the two basic swings within the golf-swing—the hand-action, allied to chipping; and the swing from the spine, allied to driving. These hand-swing and pendulum methods can be combined together in varying proportions—and in fact are hardly ever seen in their purest forms. With them, or either of them, can also be combined the method which in its purest shape is known as

*The Leo Diegel method.* This is named after a famous American professional who visited Britain with it, and came third in the Open in 1929, second in 1930, and third equal—one stroke behind Densmore Shute and Craig Wood—in 1933 (though doubtless it had been used before in Scotland, as certain old pictures suggest).

Diegel used his own version of the pendulum method, but instead of the arms being straight both were bent outwards at the elbows, with the forearms sometimes almost horizontal, and the whole resulting framework of the arms pointing at the hole. The swing was partly from the shoulders, partly from within the framework of arms.

Diegel's theory was that this method gave you a perfectly reliable swing towards the hole; and, after his repeated success, hordes of handicap golfers were to be seen 'Diegelling' on both sides of the Atlantic for some years afterwards. Hardly anyone does it now, though its traces may be seen often in older players.

*The firm-push method.* At the time of writing, this method —another old stalwart—is again in some favour in America, where a man's ability to hole six-foot putts may determine a difference of £20,000 a year in his income (no exaggeration). Like most modern American professional methods, it is extremely economical of body or shoulder movement. The arms are kept close to the body, usually with elbows comfortably relaxed against it. The club is held with the back of the left hand firmly facing the hole throughout the stroke. The club is taken back a short distance, and the ball is then pushed sharply and confidently away towards the hole, usually with only a small movement through the ball. But it can also be used successfully with a full push-follow-through towards the hole, with the club-face travelling low along the ground behind the ball, 'straight towards the hole.

It is a method seen in its purest form only on comparatively short putts—say ten feet or less. But it can work very well indeed. The theory behind it is that:

(a) It limits movement of the body—and thus avoids sway.

(b) It limits movement of the hands, and thus avoids any tendency to turn the wrists during the shot and hike the ball off the intended line.

(c) It uses the least possible general movement to get the desired result; thus cutting down *all* the possibilities of twists and jerks creeping into the stroke.

The actual stroke can be made either with the hands or the arms or with a combination of both; but it is mostly used with the left wrist held fairly firm, whatever the right is doing. Some aim the left elbow at the hole, rather Diegel-fashion.

*The strike-and-stop method.* This is another old method which looks very much like coming right back into favour at the time of writing, particularly amongst Britain's amateurs, after their once-again-chastening experience of American putting in the Walker Cup match in 1959 and in the Amateur Championship at Sandwich (where three Americans reached the semi-finals, to only one Briton, and the final was fought out between two American Walker Cup players, Hyndman and Beman—both using this method).

It has many similarities with the push method, outlined above. The stance is square and compact, with the arms and elbows relaxed and held close well into the body. But in general it is not a relaxed sort of method. It is a stiff, restricted swing at the ball—rather than a basic push. The club is swung back fairly freely and slowly, again with the back of the left wrist and hand held tautly facing the hole; but the actual stroke is more a 'strike' than a swing. (There is, in fact, nothing of 'stroke' about the stroke!)

The ball is struck—and that's the end of it! The club-face stops sharply, still facing exactly along the line. No attempt is made to give the ball the sort of true-running momentum of a swinging putt. The ball is rapped, firmly and authoritatively, at the hole; and the theory is that the hole has got to look pretty slippy if it is to jump out of the way of it!

A refinement of this method, used reputedly amongst others by that great Australian professional Peter Thomson, is to strike the ball slightly downwards, as well.

To put backspin on a putt is a physical impossibility. But it is a fact that at the hands of Thomson and others this method sometimes seemed to enable them to hit the ball a little harder, and thus make it run more certainly over the ground, while at the same time making it draw up relatively quickly for the speed it began at.

The harder you can hit any shot in golf in relation to the length needed, the more authoritatively you are able to play it. As with all putting theories, if the man who putts this way believes in it, then it works!

*The cut method.* There may or may not be a close alliance hidden away somewhere between the strike-and-stop method and the cut-it-in method, used almost since before golf began. This is very like the strike-and-stop method, especially in the curtailed follow-through and the holding of the back of the left wrist towards the hole.

But it approaches the stroke quite differently. Where the strike-and-stop method involves a perfect straight stroke at the ball (even, in isolated individual cases like that of A. D. Locke who has now won the Open five times, a stroke coming at the ball from the *inside*), the cut method involves what the name implies—a stroke in which the blade is brought across the ball from the *outside*, as in slicing cucumber.

It is even likely, since the ball is given a side-jerk towards the left at impact, that the blade must still be very slightly open to the hole (i.e. still pointing to its right) as it is brought into the ball. The effect on the ball is to send it straight for the first three-quarters at least of its run, then to curl to the right slightly as it stops. Sometimes it may not even do this, but will run straight, or scuffle straight, to a stop.

An advantage of this method is that no attempt to keep the hands rigid and square to the hole has to be made; the blade is opened naturally on the back-swing, and then stopped just after it hits the ball; and full reliance is put on relaxation and instinctive reaction to the needs of the particular putt.

It is a method to make purists wince, and selectors blench. But a few men still use it happily, and—for them—it works. It's rather a remnant of the former hickory-shafted game, and as such is worthy of a certain respect and affection.

You don't have to try it if you don't want to!

And that, of course, goes for anything anyone ever tells you about putting.

Or about golf!

# 14

# Putting under pressure

Whatever method a player uses, he still finds that when a three-foot putt really matters, or when he badly needs to hole a six-footer, his nerves betray him. The ball swims in his view. The hole swans around the green like an eccentric cog on a revolving shaft. Gremlins poke up sharp noses and whiskers at him out of the turf between him and the hole—and the noise of the worms underground is almost deafening.

His limbs alternately clench and quiver; knees quibble; eyes water; he wants suddenly to sneeze or blow his nose; he's sure there is a wasp settling on the back of his neck.

The thing begins to be difficult.

How to overcome it all?

Again, here is wide opportunity for individual experiment. Some believe that—when all this begins to happen—he must take his time over the putt, take as many little practice swings of his putter as he needs to persuade it to move more or less as usual, and then not hit the ball until he feels absolutely relaxed and happy again and confident of holing it. If necessary, get up and start all over again. This all takes some time and can leave a man exhausted, mentally, physically, and morally—especially when he subsequently still misses it.

Others believe in the 'Am-I-a-man-or-a-mouse?' approach. Golf's a game. There's a hole. Here's a ball. Knock it in. Hard luck. Good show. Good manners. Keep no one waiting. Not to make a fool of oneself about it all. 'Miss 'em quick.'

This method does at least do a great deal to improve the temper of those playing behind! Quite possibly it does little harm to the impetuous man's chances. Only one man has within living memory won the Open like that (George Duncan in 1920. He called his autobiography *Golf at the Gallop*).

The third alternative is *the repeating-drill approach*. If you want to see this in one of its most irresistible and unshakeable forms, watch Locke. Look close and long at the problem. Cogitate. Step up to ball, two little short practice sweeps, then final stance, swing back, and . . . in it nearly always goes!

Every putt of whatever length or shape gets the same treatment, the same timing in sequence. With this method, there is no question of 'Am I ready to hit it yet?' You are, by definition. You *always* are, as and when the drill leads you into the actual stroke.

Note here that a man who always walks up to his putt, takes one look at it, then strikes it first time, is as much a 'Repeating-drill' putter. *The extent and nature of the drill is up to the player.*

The essence of it is that *it is absolutely invariable*. It goes through its motions like a well-timed machine—and, having done so, leaves the rest to fate!

Every so often, the best putt in the world will miss—and part of Locke's drill is to accept this philosophically. Not quite so easy for the rest of us who haven't quite his calibre! But worth the effort.

There's also this: a putt missed counts only one stroke. Three more missed on succeeding holes, out of sheer irritation or mental confusion, make the original unlucky (or plain bad) one four times as costly!

It is no good, either, using up so much nervous energy holing crucial putts just a shade more often, if the results are exhausted drives from the following tee. This may sound far-fetched. But I myself am convinced that—especially for the ordinary week-end golfer—that *can* be the effect. Taking all things in all, the drill approach is best.

All the player can ever do, anyway, is hit the ball. The rest is up to the eternal imponderables of the game.

# 15

# Swing tonics

You have the whole golf game now. Why do we all louse it up?

We do anyway—or we'd all be potential champions. Or even play to our handicaps.

Sometimes it just goes wrong. Usually, when it is going wrong, it feels wrong, too.

There are all manner of gimmicks, reminders, and tonic ideas we can try—even in course of play.

### 1. To try when the ball is not flying straight

*Mental.* Lengthen your aim to the area beyond where the shot is to finish, i.e. don't aim at the middle of the fairway where you hope to land a drive, but at the middle of the top end—thirty yards further than you have ever driven in your life. *Don't think at all of anything in between.*

Likely effect: You'll swing right through towards the target.

*Physical.* Try to throw the club-head and/or hands out towards the point of aim as you come through on your follow-through.

Likely effect: You'll swing right through towards the target.

## 2. When hitting the ground behind the ball

*Mental.* Forget all the recent shots. Cease to be afeared. Think of yourself making the bowler leap into the air as you drive that cricket ball between his feet.

*Physical.* Aim to direct the shot low. Aim with your eye at a spot on the turf one inch in front of the ball. Anticipate the physical feel of it being picked up on the club-head as it swings down to flick through the turf at the point you are looking at. Make sure your hands have swung to a spot level with that point on the ground, before the club-head strikes the ball.

## 3. When slicing

*Mental.* Think of yourself with a grand swing that flows out through the ball towards mid-off as it comes into impact, with the hands majestically showing the way, but with the club-face square to the hole.

*Physical.* Hit as hard as hell with your right hand. (But don't, whatever you do, ease up on the left as well, or on the left elbow.)

## 4. When hooking the ball

*Mental.* Think of the ball flying up the right-hand side of the fairway with that slight shade of draw which you often see in a good club player. Expect to produce that result.

*Physical.* Try to hit the ball with the back of the left wrist and hand. Hold the whole shot up away from your body with the left arm, and make sure the left elbow is not collapsing nervously at impact. If necessary, also try turning your left hand a little bit more to the left in the address (and/or turn your right hand a little bit more over the shaft) so that the V between thumb and forefinger points well inside your right shoulder, or even towards your left eye.

## 5. Lack of length

*Mental.* As in 1 above.

*Physical.* Try to make a special point of pushing the back-swing away with your left shoulder flowing under your chin. This should both widen your back-swing arc and at the same time make sure you pivot—i.e. turn your shoulders—sufficiently to keep the arc within the plane it should lie in. And/or slow up the down-swing, or try to. This is likely to have the effect of making you hit later, and improve your timing. If your back-swing is already too slow, then speed it up a little. *The whole swing should function at an even speed.* (*See illustrations: page 49.*)

## 6. Medium iron shots going all over the place

*Mental.* Swing the club straight through the ball, and they can't help going right. See Chapter 6.

*Physical.* Remember the basic straight-left-arm swing of all iron play, and concentrate on it, sweeping left arm, wrist, and club-head back and then forward confidently at the target.

## 7. Skying the ball

*Mental.* Think of the club-head swinging straight through the back of the ball.

*Physical.* Stop poking down behind the ball. Sweep it away forward. If this fails with tee shots, lower your tee slightly and aim more at the top-back of the ball, or are you leaning back on your right foot as you hit it? Well, are you? Don't! Get the weight confidently through on to the left foot and side as you swing through the ball; and for heaven's sake let yourself go —less of this arthritic-tortoise stuff!

## 8. Topping the ball

*Mental.* 'Well, really, what a fatuous thing to do! I don't care if that happened through fanning it on the way up or fanning it on the way down. This time I'm going to sweep the club-head straight *through* the back end of the little ——!'

*Physical.* Slow down. Take your time. No hurry

**9. The quavers, the squeemy horrors**

... the quivering shakes, the ghastly certainty that you are going to foozle this shot whatever happens—just as you did the last.

*Mental.* Man, we play this game for *fun*!

*Physical.* Relax and let rip.

**10. Everything**

*Mental and Physical.* Try Ernest Jones's theory again. And try looking at the ball!

16

# Going back to the Professional

It is quite fantastically difficult for any golfer to divine what he is doing wrong himself. Quite one of the most likely dangers, if he is anything of an enthusiast and analyst of the game, is that he will be able to diagnose the immediate cause of the symptom that is afflicting him, and to attempt to apply some remedy, without having in fact got anywhere near the real root of the trouble.

Take a simple example. He finds that he has a tendency to cut his shots or else to hit them straight to the left of the target. Common sense tells him that the most likely cause of this is 'hitting from out to in', i.e. that his club-head as it comes into the ball is not—as it should be—travelling straight towards the target (or slightly towards the right of it, to straighten up as the ball is taken away) but is coming through on a line pointing to the left of it. When it does this with the face aimed roughly at the target, the result is a slice or cut. When it comes in with the club-head facing dead along its line of flight (i.e. to the left of the target), then the result is a shot that flies straight, but to the left of the intended direction.

**The full works: rotary and in-plane**

Roberto de Vicenzo, Maestro of South America's golfers about to conduct another drive 280 yards down the middle. Clubface, hands, left shoulder, ball: all lie in the same plane. A perfect position of balanced, easy, controlled generation of power into the shot, and a admirable model of how to play the game.

# The short and the long of it!

Gary Player: the little man who has worked so hard all his life to hit the ball so far, so well, so consistently.

Peter Oosterhuis: a big man with the strangely gentle method; apt occasionally to come up on the shot at the very moment he least wants to. He won the tournament Dazeley took these at, anyway and many others since.

Between them, here, these two illustrations illustrate very clearly two of the most important fundamentals of enjoying the game of golf. (Or at any rate, of

playing it well: not always quite the same thing, perhaps.)

One is the smooth rotary movement with which any good golfer swings any club.

The other is the simplicity and consistency of plane in which he swings: again with any club, for any shot, at any time.

These two characteristics of the good golf swing are the very two the dissatisfied week-end player so often hasn't ever troubled to work into his own method.

There are also two he *can* acquire, just whenever he wants to: merely by trying to – and asking his club professional to help him!

## Gary Player. 'The more I practise, the luckier I seem to get.' (*Above*)

Player has always been an indefatiguable practiser. Here you can see very clearly his consistent plane of swing. The angle at which the club-shaft inclines to the vertical in the first picture is almost exactly echoed by the angle ball-to-hands in the second: by the angle ball-hands-clubhead in the third; and by the clubshaft itself in the fourth and fifth: after the ball's away. Player strives to generate all power he possibly can from his slight stature.

## Peter Oosterhuis: power idiosyncratic. (*Below*)

Oosterhuis' address is characteristically different from the more usual straight-line-left-shoulder-clubshaft-ball. But it works for him.

As with Player, above, his bodyweight swings strongly forward into the shot: generating power as it simultaneously discharges power into the clubhead: accelerating it continuously into and through the ball.

Action sequences of Gary Player and Peter Oosterhuis at practice: *Peter Dazeley*

**Jack Nicklaus' vital example for any golfer, anywhere**

It takes a firstrate athlete (and mechanical brain) on top of form
to swing the club as Nicklaus does: in that high-elbowed wide
upright arc of his, whence comes his immense power. But here's the
secret of all his championship victories – free for any man to
borrow!
*The way he carries the power right through* the ball up into the
follow-through. In golf, nothing counts for so much as that.
(Technically, he's in fact free-wheeling at that stage; but
technicalities often only mislead us!)

Jack Nicklaus: *H. W. Neale*

If he makes a conscious effort to correct this tendency, i.e. by taking the club more 'inside' on the back-swing and pushing it 'out' on the way through, the result *may* be just satisfactory enough to make him feel he has cured his trouble. But his actual situation may very likely now become a hideous and unreliable compensatory movement for a fundamental error which is still there.

The fundamental error causing the out-to-in tendency may be something entirely simple like having his address more open (i.e. toes aligned towards the left) than is suitable for him, or it may be something a little bit more tricky like rolling out the right shoulder as he starts the back-swing, or else all manner of dubious and esoteric points of grip and sway and general approach. These he will continue with. He may even, by now, be embodying two opposite compensatory corrections, simultaneously trying to counteract two almost contradictory fundamental errors. His game will not be likely—to say the least of it —to give him much lasting pleasure. It will also be rather difficult!

The moral is, of course: 'Take it to the professional!' Take it regularly. His job is to see what is *causing* the trouble. Experience of analysing hundreds of players should have made him expert at this. But even the best of teaching professionals may quite easily be baffled at first by any individual case; he may take some time and a series of little straightening-out corrections over some weeks, to sort the whole thing out.

A custom not often practised, but invaluable to the golfer on the way up, especially the keen young player in his most formative stage of development, is to strike up an agreement with the professional—after a course of regular lessons—to come out for ten minutes or so every now and then and watch how the swing seems to be working, preferably during the hitting of a few shots on the practice ground before the weekly round begins.

The professional will then be able to encourage what is right, and gradually to help the player to eliminate what is wrong— without the formality of another course of actual lessons.

In any case, if one besetting sin seems continually to manifest itself, then that is a sure symptom that the time has come for skilled advice And it is a lamentable thing that whereas in every other phase of a successful man's life he will take (indeed he will go out of his way to seek) skilled advice in anything; in golf he will all too often persist in trying to play by the sheer light of nature—despite the fact that diagnosis is there *on the spot at the club*, awaiting the asking.

A good professional will—in these circumstances—never frighten a player by letting him know at once that the real answer is a considerable change of method. On the contrary, he will nudge the questing player towards it gradually; so cleverly, if he is a subtle fellow, that the player will firmly believe he has done it all by his own efforts, and even discovered his own errors!

If the advice has got across, and eventually been effective, *this* way, the professional will have a much more satisfied member than if he had taken him apart, spoken to him like a Dutch uncle, and made the wretched fellow scrap everything he has painstakingly worked out (he thought) for himself.

What is perhaps additionally important is that nothing will work in any golfing swing until the owner of it is really possessed of the instinctive physical knowledge of and liking for it as a method of hitting a ball. Put it there through his own mind, and the pro is doing him a great service; merely to manhandle him into the mechanics of it, and then leave him to float—often rather hopelessly—in the grip of a method he still feels is alien to him, is a recipe for producing an unhappy client. Persuasion is much more effective, in the long run at least, than dogma.

A wise pro, of course, will always be careful to praise his player for *something*. He may even invent some attribute he wants the man to have, and then gradually work him into it on the 'not quite so good that time' or the 'you must keep that (whatever it was)' approach!

Anyway, there it is; he's your man.

# 17

# The essence of the rules

The rules are beautifully written. There are far too many of them. They assume, by historic tradition, that every golfer will cheat if he is allowed the remotest opportunity to do so. They are therefore much too complicated, and often palpably unfair.

But learn them all—or at least where to track down any doubtful point (and never, of course, apply them in your favour when the *spirit* of them runs against you).[1]

Unfair they will be, and we must accept it. They have become part of the game, just like bad lies, unlucky bounces, and gremlins. After all, they will never (well, hardly ever) penalize a good shot.

Carry the little blue book in your bag. Most men players, and nearly all women players, have only the most bizarre notions of what the rules actually say on any but a commonplace point. In match-play, let your opponent's infringement ride, if it is not wilful and if it does not give him any advantage his play did not earn him.

In medal-play, though, you must speak. If you see he is going to infringe a rule, try to warn him before he does; for, if he does, you owe it to all the other competitors to take note of it. If in doubt, either of you can play out the hole with two balls, according to both of your interpretations of the right thing to do, and then submit it to the committee afterwards to decide which score counts.

It is not entirely unknown for club committees themselves to give a palpably wrong and uninformed decision; but that again is one of golf's rubs of the green. Accept their decision, then point out to one of them tactfully and privily (at least a week

[1] Apologies to any experienced golfers reading this. Beginners need to be warned of the subtleties.

later) that it ought not to establish a precedent in the club and he might look up rule so-and-so, and that if in doubt the committee might submit the matter to the R. and A. for an official decision. Golf's case-law is considerable.

The study of the rules, in fact, makes quite a fascinating side-hobby in the game; and a man who really knows them is a useful man in every club. Don't kid yourself you ever will, though. The most anyone (except the R. and A. Rules Committee) can say is: 'Well, it looks to me as if Rule X, Paragraph Y, Sub-section Z, might well apply—unless there's been a special ruling since this edition came out.'

There probably will have been—and nicely worded, too!

Rule 1, as you will have noticed, says that: '*The Game of Golf consists in playing a ball from the teeing ground into the hole by successive strokes in accordance with the rules.*' It means precisely what it says. But cases of doubt can always arise. Once after one of my wilder slices in a county championship we found the ball[1] lying neatly in a hares' set, between three young leverets—two of which were possessively cuddling it. We knew of no rule to cover the situation—except possibly in that the leverets were presumably both 'growing' and also 'adhering to the ball'.[1] My opponent sportingly and commonsensically said 'Pick and drop', which I did.

It was probably illegal! But if a point genuinely isn't covered by the rules, Rule 11, 4—the best rule in golf—comes into its own: '*If any point . . . be not covered by the rules or Local Rules, the decision shall be made in accordance with Equity.*'

It's a great pity that its application is so limited. But there it is—affirming the best of all the game's traditions.

[1] See Definition 17.

## 18

# Spin makes the ball fly

Golf is a game of controlled spin. Spin, in fact, is the very foundation of the game. Without it, it might be a game, but it would be quite a different one.

It is, indeed, spin alone that makes the flight of a golf ball possible, as we know it. Its ballistics are quite unlike those of a stone or an artillery shell. You have only to compare the fact that an artillery shell, at any strength of propulsion, will always travel its maximum distance when it is sent off at an angle of 45 degrees, with the much lower trajectory of a full drive, to appreciate the difference.

It becomes even clearer if you try to play golf without the aid of spin. You cannot well avoid putting spin on the ball, but you *can* try out a ball with a completely smooth surface—if you can get one. The result is startling. Try how you may, you cannot make it carry much further than 100 yards—usually much less. It behaves, in fact, much as a perfectly round stone would behave if sent off on the same trajectory.

This fact nearly put an end at birth to one of the most marked steps forward the game ever took—the substitution of the gutty ball for the old feathery ball. The feathery was a leather case stuffed tightly with an almost unbelievable volume of feathers, which were forced into it with a special tool. Its life was necessarily limited, especially in wet weather, and, since it was a laborious and costly thing to produce, many of the ordinary Scots of earlier times used to play golf with balls of substitute composition, and even balls carved out of wood.

Just over 100 years ago, a British golfer made a few experiments at fashioning balls out of the then new substance of gutta-percha. He merely heated up the stuff, then shaped it. The balls flew after a fashion, but were palpably inferior for easy play to the featheries, although—since all the player had to do was to melt down a damaged one again and refashion it—their lasting qualities were obvious.

Just when those who had tested them were feeling some disappointment, someone tumbled on the fact that they flew much better when they had been hacked about a bit. Once a ball was roughened, it began to hold up in the air. The tip was taken; professionals began to use moulds to make them, and soon gutties were appearing with all manner of markings on them—cross-hatching, dimples like blackberries, and all.

When the modern rubber ball came in, on the heels of the 'Haskell', makers were soon experimenting with the effects of different kinds and depths of markings. All manner of patterns were tried; and quite a series of research programmes were worked through, and are sometimes still going on; to-day most big manufacturers have their own ball-driving machines, for calibration purposes.

What exactly is behind this?

In general, practically every shot in golf is actually hit with backspin. Since the club-face is not perfectly straight, but is 'lofted', e.g. set at less than a right angle to the horizontal, the direction of the blow will not be straight through the middle of the ball from its first circumferential point of impact with the surface of the club-face, but it will be imparted *from* that point through the ball *below* its centre of gravity.

The ball will fly away from the club-face roughly at right angles to the face. But the angle of the blow, directed below the centre of the ball, will spin that bottom half forward, as the upper half—not so quickly in contact with the club-face—lags behind.

The result is a 'backspin', with the ball spinning forward on its underneath side, and backward on its top side.

Common sense would suggest that as the ball flies thus spinning through the air, with the bottom side trying to drag air forward with it *against the main flow*, and the top side spinning *with the main flow*, the extra pressure generated underneath it would tend to hold it up in the air. Common sense would, as a matter of fact, be talking the most arrant rubbish, since the real reasons are rather more subtle and complicated. The general effect, though, is exactly as expected.

How big this lifting effect is, depends upon two things: the speed of spin, and the depth of surface markings.

Since, with us, the depth of surface markings is fixed from the moment we buy our ball (as is size: 1·62 inches diameter, and weight: 1·62 ozs.), it doesn't come into play at all. But it is interesting to check for a moment how the present depths are chosen. (It applies equally to the American 1·68-inch size.)

In general, the deeper the markings the greater the lifting effect from the same amount of spin. Some of the pre-war balls, with deep, rectangular markings, 'took such a good grip on the air' that a well-hit shot would often soar way up—losing length as it did so.

On the other hand, it gave the player every opportunity to put plenty of spin on the ball exactly as he wanted, when he wanted it. Had it not also given him plenty of spin on every hook or slice he put on the ball accidentally, it might have lasted longer in favour! (And there is a school of thought, to which the author subscribes enthusiastically, which holds that golf would be a better, more skilful, and more amusing game even than it is, if the ball were to be made a little larger and lighter, and minimum depths of marking laid down which would ensure plenty of healthy spin on the ball—whether intentional or not. The characteristics of shots would be the more clear and emphatic in the ball's behaviour, and the possibilities of putting desired spin on the ball to produce desired results would be very much increased. It would also be less of a strain to hit.)

The present depths of markings are the compromise chosen by each manufacturer, almost entirely with the idea of making the average player happy, by providing the amount of spin effect which will make the ball go as far as possible from his drive.

There are slight variations between ball and ball. A weak hitter, who has difficulty in making the ball travel, might well be advised to try several makes in a seriously questing spirit, including the tough, square-marked 'Kro-Flite', before deciding which ball flies best *for him*. Any larger American-size ball is much easier to strike, for instance.

With marking depth and spin characteristics taken as given, though, there still remain the possibilities of applied spin.

Obviously, the more loft there is on a club, the more at an angle to the ball's surface the true direction of the blow becomes, and the more spin is imparted to the ball in relation to its speed of flight.

A niblick can be made to put so much spin on a ball that, on landing, it will actually jump backwards. A straight-faced driver, at the other extreme, puts the minimum spin on the ball—just enough to make it hold up in the air to produce its maximum length of flight for the maximum drive.

But the spin imparted by every shot depends also upon the way the player, intentionally or unintentionally, hits it. Obviously if he hits it with his driver's face open, and coming into the ball bottom edge leading, thus increasing the loft, he will not only send the ball off on a higher trajectory, he will put more spin on it too.

If he also (or alternatively) pokes down through the shot·so that the club-face, instead of swinging straight forward towards the lowest point of the swing, is being jabbed downwards across the back of the ball as well, then a lot more extra spin will go on; the result will be one of those high irritating soaring shots, that the player so often cannot begin to imagine the cause of. (Next time, he jabs down even harder, puts even more spin on it, and it soars even more! Strangely enough, to keep his ball down to the desired height of flight, this player would need to make a point of trying to make himself draw the club up a little through impact.)

More confusion in the mind of the player arises purely because the whole game of golf is cocked over at an angle. He understands easily that, if he draws the face of the club across the ball from out to in, then he will spin the left-hand side of it forward and the result will be a slice—a ball curving in its flight towards the right. He understands equally well that, if he pushes the face of the club across the ball from in to out, then he is spinning the right-hand side of the ball forward, and the ball will curve away as a hook, leftwards in its flight.

What he often doesn't quite get clear is that—owing to the sheer fact that he is addressing the ball, and swinging at it, at an angle from the 'pull side'—it is quite easy to cut across it, heel first from out to in, in such a way as to increase the vertical component of the spin, the backspin, far more than any horizontal component, or slice-spin.

In fact, as any player knows, this nearly always does happen on a slice—and the result is a high flying ball, with increased backspin effect as well as the curve to the right; while the skilled player can 'cut one up' without putting much slice-curve on it.

(The two components of spin, vertical and horizontal, do, of course, always function as one spin on an angle between their two theoretical axes, but it is much easier to think of it as if they did not, as if they existed as two spins in the vertical and horizontal planes respectively.)

Contrarily, when the opposite spin is put on, that produced by pushing the face of the club across the ball away from the feet, to produce the hook, the flight is often a lower one than usual, simply because the hooking effect tends to reduce the backspin component. The ball, as well as turning to the left in the air, flies low and runs like anything when it lands. The extreme example of this is when the ball is given so much hook-spin, cancelling out so much of the normal backspin, that it becomes what is known as a 'quick hook'—doubling to ground again very like a completely smooth ball, and diving straight for the nearest rabbit hole.

There's here a bit of ridiculously irrelevant, but practical, observation of things as they are which might be worth noting.

It's simply this. All Club Committees slice!

What's that got to do with ballistics? Simply that on most courses, most of the time, the rough to the *right* of the hole is kept well under control by the Greens Staff, with any bushes, etc, ball-findable-in. Because that's where the Committee go.

So anyone who cares to opt to pay less (other things being equal) for crooked shots is wiser to cultivate a swing in which anything going haywire with any stroke results far more likely in a fade or cut, than in a draw or hook. Faders *may* not hit the ball so far from the tee. But they do tend to score better: on most courses, anyway. (And in fact usually strike the ball more consistently, since a fade is easier to control than a draw).

So much for the general picture. We should now get down to some more precise analysis of the place of spin in the game.

## 19

# The ten crooked shots of golf

The basic shots using sidespin are again best learnt from a professional—abetted by your close watching of him when he does it himself, and by your observation of how your fellow players produce unintentional hooks and slices during play. I strongly advise anyone who really wants to *tackle* golf to take this trouble. The professional will be quite prepared to show you how to do them both, and to devote a couple of lessons to coaching you in producing them at will. With them as measuring rods, you can better assess all the involuntary benders that beset us.

As a ready reference and reminder afterwards, here are the basics of them: *Quick hook, left hook, pull, hook, draw, fade, cut, push, slice, super-slice.*

On page 85 in simple diagram are the mechanics of benders.

I have given them in their pure forms. They rarely appear so simple and clear-cut as this, since many bad shots combine one or more of them. But their essence is simple; and from it stem their effects.

The names I have given to them are sometimes used loosely; we are all criminals here, in overlapping their senses. Golf writers particularly are prone to loose terms, myself by no means least. If you do not actually see the club come into the ball, and may not get a clear view of it from behind or in front, but only see where it ends up, and maybe the last part of its flight, you cannot conceivably know which *exactly* it was—and the reader certainly doesn't care.

So the placing of names to the examples given here may be marginally arguable. I believe they are the correct ones for identifying the separate types of off-line or spun shots—all of which are emphatically separate and real entities.

Note a few essentials:

## 1. The straight shot, the pull, and the push

These are identical in one respect; they are the only ones in which at impact the club-head is *correctly aligned at right angles to its direction of travel.*

All three, therefore, fly dead straight. But in two of them the club-head is swinging *in the wrong direction* at impact, as a result of swing error. Out-to-in, with face square to direction of swing, produces a *pull.* In-to-out, with face square to direction of swing, produces a *push.*

The man who hits either of them, therefore, can be sure that in this respect his stroke has been precise; and if he is continually doing it, then all he has to do is to check on his stance, aim, and actual direction of swing, until he manages to swing straight and produce a straight shot. (Warning: *But* they may all, including the straight shot, be produced by a combination of errors; and one of these errors, found and corrected, may suddenly leave the others free to produce shots that do not fly straight at all— to the desperation and fury of the player. Straight to a professional, then; you're in trouble.)

## 2. The hook and the cut

These are similarly true brothers. These terms are properly used for the shot which the player sends off line without meaning to, which begins *straight* and then curves away off the line. In both of them the face is square to the target at impact, but not square to the line of flight of the club-face. The hook swing comes across from in to out through impact, the cut from out to in.

As in the pull and push, it is the *direction of swing* that is at fault, and, since this time the swing is not at right angles to the

# HOW THE BENDS BEGIN

X is taken to be the angle by which the club-face is turned away from the straight line to the hole at impact in a normal slice.

For simplicity of exposition, in the eight cases where the actual direction of swing through impact itself diverges from the straight line to the hole, it is shown as doing so by this same X. This is in fact just about typical of what actually happens.

| | | |
|---|---|---|
| SDS | | Club-face pointing square to the direction of the swing, i.e. exactly at 90° to it. |
| SH | | Club-face pointing square to the hole, i.e. at exactly 90° to the right line. |
| L | $\frac{1}{2}$X | Club-face pointing left of the line to the hole, by one-half the angle-off of swing shown for the four at the left. |
| L | X | Club-face pointing left of the line to the hole, by exactly the angle-off of swing shown for the four at the left. |
| L | $1\frac{1}{2}$X | Club-face pointing left of the line to the hole, by $1\frac{1}{2}$ times the angle-off of swing shown for the four at the left. |
| R | $\frac{1}{2}$X | Club-face pointing right of the line to the hole, by one-half the angle-off of swing shown for the four at the right. |
| R | X | Club-face pointing right of the line to the hole, by exactly the angle-off of swing shown for the four at the right. |
| R | $1\frac{1}{2}$X | Club-face pointing right of the line to the hole, by $1\frac{1}{2}$ times the angle-off of swing shown for the four at the right. |

### NOTES

With L$\frac{1}{2}$X and R$\frac{1}{2}$X, the club-face is pointing halfway between the hole and the direction of swing.

With L$1\frac{1}{2}$X and R$1\frac{1}{2}$X, the club-face is pointing one-half wider still than the angle between direction of swing and line to the hole.

Hook, Left Hook, and Quick Hook all begin from the club-face aiming left of the direction of swing at impact. The difference in behaviour between them arises from their respective directions of swing. The true Hook starts off straight, the Left Hook starts off left of target, the Quick Hook left of everything. The Draw, on the other hand, begins right of target.

Precisely the same relationship, in reverse, exists between Cut, Slice, and Super-Slice; and the Fade begins left of target.

The Pull and the Push can be just straight shots which aren't looking where they are going. But they can be the result of two simultaneous errors. They are also, of course, all too easy to produce when playing for a Draw or a Fade.

The Shank and Reverse Shank, being just misses, are not shown—thank goodness.

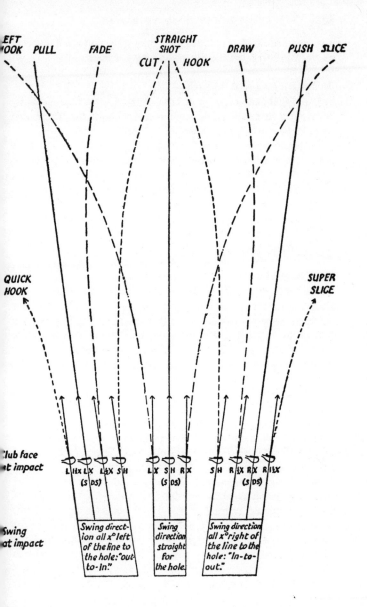

alignment of the face, the result will be spin, and a ball curving away in the air from the line upon which it begins.

### 3. The left hook and the slice

The visual characteristic of both of these is that they actually *begin* on a line to left and right respectively of the target, *and* bend further away from it as they proceed.

In their pure theoretical form (which, again, does not always appear in pristine simplicity), they have two things in common. One is that the swing itself is straight on target. The other is that at impact the club-face is pointing, not at the target, but substantially to one side or the other of it.

In either case, since it is not facing at right angles to the direction in which the club-head is travelling, spin will be imparted to the ball.

### 3a. The quick hook and the super-slice

These are identical in origin with the hook and the slice. But added to their troubles is the fact that not only is the club-face pointing respectively left or right of the line of swing, but the line of swing itself is also off-aim in the same direction. The quick hook is thus, as it were, a left hook superimposed on a pull; the super-slice a slice superimposed on a push. The results are horrible, as we all know.

In the case of the quick hook, it will set off in the direction in which the club-face is pointing, that is, to the left of both line of swing and target, and—with this flying start in the wrong direction—will then bend further away ferociously and dive into trouble about 150 yards from the tee; much less than the normal distance of a straight shot with the same club.

Both these characteristics, the sharp bend on the ball, and the lack of carrying capacity, are due to the reduced component of backspin, caused by the fact that this player is (as on every shot) swinging the club from the pull side anyway, and by turning the club-face that way also reduces the loft on it, while the large hook-spin component turns the axis of spin of the ball towards the plane player's-eye-to-ball, thus 'wrapping it down'.

In the super-slice, on the other hand, the correspondingly

large component of spin in the opposite direction, coupled with the fact that the club-face, being aimed to the right of both the target and the line of swing, must also be turned more up in the air, thus increasing backspin, sends the ball off right of target with an axis of spin cocked away over towards a *right angle* to the plane player's-eye-to-ball. The result is a ball that not only bends enthusiastically further and further right, but tends to soar up into the sky as well, and, having travelled very much less than the usual distance of a straight shot with the same club, flops to earth exhausted with itself.

Where the quick hook is wrapped down *within* the swing-arc's angle, the super-slice is floated up at a tangent to it.

There is thus—contrary to centuries of invocations from centuries of golfers—no mystery at all about why the quick hook and the super-slice behave as they do, nor why the quick hook will try to run on landing, while the super-slice will settle into the heather like treacle into a pancake. It's all in the elementary ballistics of the player's hitting approach to the ball, coupled with the doubled errors he is making.

To understand how these things happen, is to take a big step towards being able to correct a tendency to any of them as it comes along. (And to see why upright swingers often produce higher hooks and lower slices than flat swingers.)

## 4. The draw and the fade

These have this in common: both are intentional; and the club-face is aimed at impact somewhere between *square to the hole* and its *direction of travel*. For instance—the golfing craftsman may play his intentional fade with the club-face aligned slightly left of the target at impact, so that, while his swing cuts slightly across the ball from out to in, the slighter 'pull' alignment of the face produces a reduced fading effect and makes sure of starting the ball left. Vice versa with the draw.

In the normal fade and draw, also, the hands determinedly hood[1] the face through impact; that is, the player reduces its effective loft by having his hands well in front of the club-head at impact to produce the low, under-control shot usually best.

[1] For practical method of hooding, see next chapter.

REMINDER CODE.          Club-face shut, swing out-to-in—straight pull.

Club-face shut, swing straight on target—left hook, starting left.

Club-face open, swing in-to-out—straight push.

*Using 'shut', 'open', and 'square' all in relation to line to target, not to line of swing.*

Club-face open, swing straight on target—slice, starting right.

Club-face square, swing out-to-in—cut, starting straight.

Club-face square, swing in-to-out—hook, starting straight.

Club-face slightly shut and hooded, swing out-to-in—controlled low fade, starting slightly left.

Club-face slightly open and hooded, swing in-to-out—controlled low draw, starting slightly right.

Don't be afraid to try them all. They are great fun: so long as the practice ground is wide enough!

### Variations of controlled draw and controlled fade
Both these can be played higher than usual, for any reason which appeals to the player, by combining the general technique for them given above, with the address and approach for a high shot given a few pages later on. Both can also be played unusually low, e.g. into a wind or under a wind, by using the general stance set up for a low shot.

### The shank, socket, or off-the-pipe shot
Not really a golf shot at all, but simply, like the top, the sclaff, the heel, or the toe, a species of miss. The ball is not struck cleanly with the face of the club but against the edge of the shaft or socket. It usually flies over point or mid-off; occasionally—hit with the under-side of the shank—it flies back past your feet towards mid-on. The swing and club-face may have been perfectly aligned in everything except their application to the ball!

# 20

# Making use of spin

The good player can use these spin effects to produce what he wants. Not just the simple hook and slice to bend round a tree or other obstruction, but also for controlling the behaviour of the ball on a more or less straight shot.

## The draw
Perhaps the simplest example is that low, running, controlled draw. A good player can propel it in such a way that it sets off over the right-hand side of the fairway with a low flight, comes in towards the middle as it falls to earth, and then runs a very much longer way than usual. He may use this, for instance, against a left-hand wind; or even with a wind coming hard over the slips, to give himself an extra-long drive.

It is also possible, though, by combining the in-to-out move-ment across the face of the back of the ball, with a slightly open club-face and a firmly downwards blow, to combine a hook spin with a strong backspin effect on landing. The South African professional (and four times Open Champion) Bobby Locke does this the whole time—he hardly ever plays a shot any other way. It works for him because he enjoys hitting the ball that way, and finds he can do it most consistently. It is, though, something of a master-technique, not easily within the skill of the average performer!

## The fade
Similarly, that basic fade. The player hits the shot with his hands well ahead of the ball and the club-face hooded. The ball sets off low along the left-hand side of the fairway, and then just eases into the middle towards the end of its flight. Ben Hogan, probably the greatest of all American professionals, used this

consistently at one time—and had many imitators amongst players of some ability who had been beset with hooking troubles.

The thing to note here is that with many variations of intentional spin, used purely for the sake of putting the ball in a definite position on fairway or green (either to guard against a player's own besetting error, or to guard against a particularly disastrous hazard on any particular hole), the thing is much more safely done with the hands rather more ahead of the ball than usual, and the club-face hooded.

This is partly because the result is a more crisp, emphatic, authoritative stroke, and partly because, where you are being bold enough to spin a shot, it is usually safer to keep it on a fairly low trajectory, which will incidentally make sure you get the full length out of whatever club you are able to use.

This concept of 'hooding' the club is a very important one for the improving player to get clear. It is best learnt by individual experiment. Take, for instance, a 6-iron, and address the ball in the stance the professional will have taught you—feet square or slightly open, ball just forward of the middle of the feet. Now push the ball back along the line of flight (or very slightly inside it, i.e. along the club-head's arc of swing) away from the hole, to a position level with the right heel; do this without moving the feet, and *keep the hands in the same position* as they were for the normal address; just move the club-face back and address the ball in the new position.

You will probably have opened the club-face in so doing, so that it now points to the right of the line of play. Correct this, and place it square to the line (and, probably, find that you must adjust your hands slightly by pulling them in towards your body to make the club sit square on the ground, before this new position feels comfortable; or maybe you may feel you must lower them slightly).

You are now in the position to play a hooded 6-iron shot. It may help if you relax your knees just a little more than you do with a normal shot, or hold the club just a little bit nearer the top end of the grip, or crouch a little more on the shot—or any combination of all three. With the club-face pointing, as you have placed it, *exactly in the same direction as before,* and your hands well in front of it at the address, so that the shaft, seen from your eye, slopes backwards towards the ball, you will see that the club-face is lying at the ball in very much the position of loft of a 5-iron played at normal position.

This will not of course give you the same shot as a 5-iron. It will give you a low-flying shot, with more backspin than you usually get on a 5-iron, because of the downward blow through the ball, and sometimes more than on a 6-iron. The take-up of the ball will be crisper, the divot slightly bigger, and the follow-through probably slightly shorter. Obviously this way of playing a shot will force the ball more certainly out of a tight lie, a divot mark, or a downhill lie—or any lie where there is some obstacle o taking the ball away completely cleanly.

But it can equally easily be used off a clean lie, or a thick grassy lie, just to produce a crisp, low-flying, biting shot. It is very useful indeed for playing up to the pin against the wind, whether a full shot or half-shot (an old-fashioned poke), with any club. It also makes it easier—if the method feels comfortable to you—to make sure of playing the ball straight and making it fly straight. Not only is there less chance for wind to get hold of the ball, but also the flight of the ball will be lower, and thus the run straighter, and less affected by bumps on the pitch, than in an ordinary stroke.

## The high cut

The tendency of the common or garden unwanted slice to send the ball high, with lots of stop, can also be harnessed to the player's stroke-making. By addressing the ball from a position slightly more behind it than usual, and bringing the stroke more under the back of the ball, with the club-face *slightly* open to the line of the stroke (but *not* to the line of aim), the ball can be made to fly higher than is usual for that particular club, and—probably, but depending upon other conditions—stop more quickly too.

The points to note about the technique of this stroke can be summed up as follows:

Stance: Open, i.e. left foot drawn back from the line right toe to target and the toe turned slightly more than usual towards the target. This stance helps to make it natural to draw the club-face across under the ball very slightly from out to in. (Note that, for a possible cause of involuntary slicing!)

Both feet, and the stance in general, must move round the ball also towards the rear, i.e. if the ball is at the centre of the clock-face and the line to the target is at nine o'clock then the general mean-stance position moves round from six o'clock to five-thirty or even to five o'clock. The ball is thus left further in front of the player's body, in relation to the line of the target, than in a normal stance.

Having taken up this stance, and adjusted the grip so that, with the hands and club-head lying in the normal position in relation to the stance, the club-face points again at the target, the next point is—strangely and contradictorily enough—*not* to take the club back outside the line. For what you have already done is to move yourself to a position where the whole swing of the ball will be tangential anyway. Just, therefore, try to swing the club back from the target—in the normal arc in relation to it—and then down and through, and the effect will (or should) be to give you a high, cutting shot, starting just left of the target and flying across to land and bounce into it from the left.

As a matter of fact, a little experience with this method will enable you to give the ball the height you want combined with exactly as much slice or cut as you want—depending largely on how far ahead of the club-head the hands are at impact. You can also, by bringing the swing from the inside-to-out angle, but with the same cutting-under technique, send it dead straight or even with a slight draw, despite its height and stopping spin. (You can also, if you get the club-head in too soon—i.e. catching up with your hands before the ball is struck—produce the most disastrous pull, or even in nervous cases a terrible quick hook; moreover, if you lag back on the shot, and slightly toe it, it can give you a slice right in the other direction.)

This all sounds frightening; but golf is like that all the time! Changes of stance, grip, and approach will never produce the shot you want unless you also hit it in the way you want to hit it. All they can do is to set you into the easiest position and approach from which to play the shot you intend to play.

There is nothing sacred about anything in golf. In the essence, what hits the ball is the craftsmanlike action of the hands. You can, if you are skilful and experienced, stand for a hook and play a slice, or stand for a cut-up shot and play a low hook, you can even drive with your legs crossed if you like, but it doesn't make it any easier. Standing the most comfortable way does.

## Straightforward high shot with extra backspin

This one also involves spin, but less complicatedly (and perhaps less dangerously so) than the high cut. It merely consists of what a boy does when throwing stones. Try it.

Pick up a stone (or a ball) and aim to throw it horizontally. Note how your shoulders are set—about horizontal too. Now aim to throw a high one: your shoulders will correspondingly have instinctively altered their position, and set themselves to point towards the angle you intend to throw the ball, left shoulder high, right shoulder low.

You can, to a certain extent, modify the height of your golf shots in this same simple way. For a high one the hips stay in very much the same relative position to the ball at the address as for any other shot; but the body sets back away from the target from the waist, to fall in with the cocked-up angle of the shoulders; and the whole swing follows the line of the shoulders.

Similarly, to play a low shot, set the body more forward towards the hole from the hips, to agree with the horizontal aim of the shoulders, and swing at the ball correspondingly lower and straighter towards the target (the old idea of making the bowler jump in the air to avoid the ball sizzling between his feet).

As a general and realistic guide—if you imagine a man standing ten yards away: to play a high shot, set your aim to play over his head: to play a low shot, set your aim to play between his knees.

Note here, that, although the low shot will help you to get the ball up from a tightish lie, the high shot—played straight like this—becomes much more difficult if the ball is lying low or if there is a lump behind it, and recourse must then be had once more to the cut-up method.

## General

The cut-up method can, in fact, be used for all manner of other shots as well as high ones. It can be used to force the ball up from a thick lie; it can be used—more, it emphatically *should* be used—to lift the ball from a down-slope when plenty of carry is still needed in the air before the ball pitches on the green. A perfect example of this is the drive that ends on a down-slope, and leaves the player with a shot to carry a line of bunkers which he could fairly easily carry with a straight shot from the level, but not at all surely with a straight shot played with the axis of the swing adjusted for the down-slope.

One tip may help here. If you have difficulty in making the ball rise, or want to reduce the amount of cut, fade, or slice in the air, it helps many players if the left hand is moved slightly over the top of the shaft towards the right (keeping the right hand where it is). It helps others to keep the grip the same, but concentrate on making this turning movement during the back-swing, with the club-head turning correspondingly: i.e. rolling shaft and club-head over together. The result is lots of left wrist cock at the top of the swing, and more of a definite bite upwards in the shot at impact.

This, though, is all rather advanced technique; controversial and depending on a number of other variables in your personal swing-characteristics. There's nothing to stop you trying it; but overdo it and you'll find yourself flying to the left of the target, instead of into it.

These are all shots which will increase the possible satisfaction of golf. They are all shots, too, which only you yourself can teach yourself to play in the end.

If you are really keen on this fascinating and rewarding aspect of golf, then to be able at will to slice and hook, at least, is essential. The professional may here suggest that it might be better first to learn how to hit the ball straight! But most amateurs never do that all the time, if only because they are never completely in practice; and, if a man knows how to play the benders, then he knows not only how he's likely to be producing them accidentally, but how to guard against doing it again.

# 21

# Advanced chipping

Let's now have a close and critical look at what might be called 'advanced chipping'.

## Aim to lay it dead

Strangely enough, whatever the lie and whatever lies in between you and the hole, it is nearly always possible to lay the ball dead.

Often it will look difficult. But it will be possible. The great thing is never to be so afraid of the look of the thing, and the obvious possibilities of foozling or doing something else stupid with it, that you fail to attempt to play the shot in the best possible way.

[Obviously there must be exceptions here, identifiable by common sense. If your opponent has played 6 and is in a bunker, while you have played 2 and are in the rough with a large bunker between you and the hole, which lies only ten feet beyond it, and with a stream over the back of the green—you don't go straight for the hole; you take three or even four more shots safely to win the hole. And if you have three shots for the monthly medal, when just off the 18th green, that is no time to try anything clever, if a safe alternative presents itself.

Note, though, while we're still in the brackets, that more holes are lost and chances thrown away through amateurs trying to be sensible and 'play safe' than through any other way. Put your ball right away on the safe side of the green, and the long putt suddenly looks frightening in its turn. It's very much a matter of temperament. Personally I like to see a man go for it—and keep his head down; the shot will still leave him in a comparatively safe position unless it is completely muffed or miscalculated—and there's no need to do that. Often, to trust your judgement and play the shot boldly is the safest possible alternative.]

## Certain chipping

There is one rule that goes for nearly all chips, flips, and short pitches, whatever angle and lie they may be played from. That is: there must be that crisp forward movement through the ball, picking it up on the way down to bottom-dead-centre of the swing, even if only infinitesimally so. Now this does not mean that the club-head must always be travelling downwards when it hits the ball. Far from it; you may be in a position from which you want a sharply rising flip from an uphill lie; in this case the whole axis of the shot will be cocked over away from the hole; so that, although the club must be coming towards bottom-dead-centre of the swing on its own cocked-back axis, it may actually be coming upwards as it hits the ball, in relation to true horizontal. (Remember the boy with the stone.)

Here again, maybe, is work for your already acquired acquaintance, the cut-up shot. You want the ball to go almost vertically upwards, flip over an obstacle on to the green, and stop quickly. You must hit the ball true, for plenty of stop, with the usual downward swing in relation to the angle of aim. But you will never in thousands of years get a ball to rise almost straight upwards by hitting down in relation to the horizontal. If the lie allows you to cock the axis of the swing backwards, away from the hole, fine. If it doesn't, then you must improvise.

## Improvise

Improvisation, in fact, is the key to advanced chipping and pitching. If you still want that same sharply rising and quickly stopping ball (to flip, for instance, over a bunker and stop quickly on the other side of it), but your lie is too flat to allow for any considerable cocking-up of the swing, then you must approach it a different way.

You know from experience how anything hit at an angle to the striking arc will impart spin! If you have played tennis at some time, you will be familiar with the sort of cut-across-and-under back-hand shot which chugs up weakly over the net, but then bounces back again to the side it was first played from, before anyone has a chance of reaching it (much used by schoolboys—who have never been taught to play tennis properly—

against their sisters, who have been and resent it).

Here is an occasion when you want the same sort of effect from golf. So play the same shot. It's a hands' movement. Cut across the ball and under it—'Flip its gaiters off'—(but taking it still before bottom-dead-centre) with lots of right-hand action and a quickly rising follow-through immediately after the ball is hit.

Above all, the thing to remember in this sort of situation, about the mechanics of the golf swing, is this.

The left hand must *lead* firmly through the stroke, if it's to work to best effect. So the more the player thinks of the *back* of the left hand and wrist swinging together through the shot decisively towards the hole, the more likely any stroke will be to come off accurately.

Nearly every shot of this kind fluffed in golf (including those fluffed by highly skilled professionals in the Open!) is fluffed through this simple, but absolutely fundamental, mechanical rule being broken: at least in some degree.

The other thing the player has particularly to watch, of course, is that he (or she) doesn't—by sheer excess of delicacy and finessemanship (or womanship)—understrike the shot!

Few things in golf are much more totally exasperating (not least to your partner in a foursome, who may all too downrightly be your wife) than the beautifully played stroke, describing a perfect parabola—to end just not *quite* over the bunker it had to clear to be any use at all!

This is one of the classic 'Tiger-Fluffs' of the game.

Its effect upon morale (not least your opponents') is straight to the belly. It is the easiest thing in the world to do.

It must, though, be a *swing*, in perfect rhythm. Here is a moment when 'swing the club-head' becomes absolutely more essential perhaps than at any other. Any sort of a jab will be fatal—or will at least deserve to be. Any attempt to have the bottom of this little flipping, cutting swing *behind* the ball will lead to either a complete fluff, or else a thinly hit one going too far and not stopping, or, worst of all and unfortunately only too likely, a straightforward solid stroke—hit smack off the front of the club's cutting edge—which flies straight across the green like lightning and into trouble on the other side.

There must be a distinct and perfect 'Flip' exactly as you hit the ball. This is timing, and is the only way to time the shot. Don't poke. Don't hit. Swing the club-head with the hands, on to, under, and through the ball.

### Toe through, or face held

There are two variations of this shot. One is the straightforward one in which the wrists work normally as in a long shot, and the club-face already points to the left of the hole when knee-high on the follow-through. The other is the sometimes more reliable one—particularly when cutting under the ball—in which the club-head comes in open and is then held square to the hole as the follow-through begins. In other words, the cutting action of the right hand across and under the ball is arrested at impact with a holding of the face, and a swinging-through of the blade with its face towards the hole. (*See illustration: page 81.*)

All these can also be played with stiff wrists and an arm-swing from the shoulders, instead of a hand-swing from the fingers; but this is really rather difficult—and (although perhaps the biggest backspin effect of all can be produced this way) I would not advise trying this *until you can do it the easier way first*.

The 'feel' in the hands is prime, and must come first. Stance is up to you. But, the more you want to cut the ball up and spin it, the more easy will you find it to play the shot if your feet are open in relation to each other, and both cocked round to the left.

A useful basic guide, upon which you can work your own variations, is to have the ball at a position level with your left toe, or even just ahead of it; with your *left* foot at the *angle* of the hour hand at seven o'clock, your *right* at its *angle* at eight o'clock (in relation to the hole at twelve o'clock), and their *positions* such that a line from right toe to left toe would pass very well left of the hole—anything up to an angle of 45 degrees from the direct line to it.

The more sharply you want to lift the ball, the more you want to turn your feet and whole stance to the left; the less you want to lift it, the less you want to turn your stance, and the further back you can place the ball. You can still get good loft and maximum control of spin with the ball in a position just opposite your right toe (and thus slightly in advance of your right heel, due to the way the foot is turned).

## Getting the ball up neatly

The actual cut is produced more by the position and approach of the club-face than by any actual swing across the line. Many players actually take the club back in such a way that, as it reaches the horizontal on the little back-swing from the hands, the shaft is actually pointing through the hands directly at the hole, with the toe (or even the face) of the blade pointing upwards at the sky. Then, on the swing-down, the club-face comes in markedly heel first, with the bump of the heel touching the ground first and the whole face swinging into the position where it directly faces the hole only as (or even after) the ball is taken.

To a beginner this may sound quite lunatic. Try it. If it doesn't work, you are doing something wrong. But you'll soon get the feeling of floating the ball up in the air this way, and soon begin to get the measure of how minute variations in action and strength determine range and height and spin.

Only practice and experiment can make you master of this type of shot (which is, incidentally, very closely allied to one type of shorter bunker flip used most effectively by American professionals).

I have gone into this shot at perhaps immoderate length, because it is the basis of many other shots around the green.

The same sort of shot, but played more downwards, either with the swing axis cocked forward, or with more intentional and conscious downbite in the club-head, will yet enable you to play an accurate shot out of a rough lie, to bite the ball at least safely out of a bare lie, and to make it rise from a downhill one.

It is, as experience will show, a *strong* sort of shot. It can even be used with a fair hope of complete success out of a downhill lie in heather. So when you find yourself under the rim of an anthill, or lodged in the thick slope of a bunker of some declivity facing the pin, here is the one to try.

Delicacy of touch will come with practice. And, using this kind of technique, it is even possible to make a shot fly low out of thick grass and pull up as if on a string on the surface of a baked-hard green.

### A forcing chip

Another type of approach stroke is the hooded-faced hook. This is, of course, precisely the opposite approach in every way to the various forms of cut we have just considered. It can be very useful out of a bad or rough lie.

Where the last one was played with the heel of the club coming in first, this one is played with the toe coming in first and definitely *taking* the ball. The stance this time feels most comfortable if square or slightly shut, with the ball back towards, or even behind, the level of the right foot. The club is taken back comfortably inside the line to the hole, so that when the shaft reaches the horizontal it is pointing through the hands roughly towards mid-off, or even deep cover, and not opened at all, so that the face is facing directly at the ball, or at a point on the ground just the other side of it, on the line from your right foot.

As the club-head swings back again, the toe bites first through the grass and begins to take up the ball, which is gripped more and more towards the centre of the face as the club comes through.

The hands must, usually, of course, be well ahead of the club-head at impact; and—as with the cut-up shot—you can either play this shot with a sharp, crisp, decisive roll-through of the right hand, or else play it with an arrested hooking action, and swing the face of the club through low and still facing towards the hole.

As it comes into the ball it should still be facing a shade to the right of the target, but swinging into a position facing the target as the ball is taken up.

This is much less of a swinging-flip sort of shot than the cut-up. It can be as firm as you like, and can even be played as a push or a shove (or a chop) with the hands.

The advantage of it is in its ability to force the ball—in *control* —out of thick grass or rough. For best purposes you want a rather round club-face for it, and not too much flatness on the bottom. You may have a niblick like this, but you may find it more effective to use your 7-iron.

In short run-up shots, where an attempt to run up simply with a mashie might prove unpredictable out of the grass (you can never quite tell how much it will arrest either ball or club-head), with practice you will come to feel that this hooded, sharp-hooking method is pretty reliable—and you know exactly what the ball will do if you hit it as you mean to.

It is also a useful shot against the wind, where you want to make sure of getting up to the hole, without having to baste the ball too hard with a straight-faced club, giving lots of run.

There will be spin on this sort of shot; and there should be enough to make it skid on the first bounce and begin to pull up on the second, without ever rising much in the air at all.

# 22

# Temperament

**Don't muck yourself up. Leave that to golf—it needs remarkably little help**

Golf is a game of the mind.

To any non-golfer watching golf this may seem an odd statement. To many golfers, who have long noticed that tournament winners amongst the professional ranks do not always appear —at least outwardly—anything but phlegmatic, it may seem even odder.

But it is true, in two ways. First it is true in the need for craftsmanship, for intelligent use of the physical senses. This all outstanding players command.

Secondly it is a game of resolution and determination—which any man has within him to draw upon.

But thirdly it is also a game in which the imaginative can suffer agonies of self-destruction and self-torture: the comparative immunity to which (it is sometimes unkindly and, I think, inaccurately alleged) accounts for the success of many *apparently* stolid fellows. It does not prevent the successes of many exceptionally clever characters as well—but they have to work harder to achieve self-control and go through greater agonies in doing so. The outwardly phlegmatic mien conceals much stress within!

Any beginner who has got this far in this book is certainly in for it!

The mental component in golf lends itself to categorical headings.

### 1. Tendency to blind fury

Golf is potentially, and often in fact, the most irritating game on earth. A man who may be a complete master of his life's career, a don, a managing director, a minister of Church or State, a head postmaster, a distinguished surgeon, a successful greengrocer, a skilled plasterer, a king bricklayer (or even a writer!), may find himself faced with the simple proposition of knocking a ball some twenty yards with a club (for which he has paid something over £4) on to a green as large as a cricket pitch—and he foozles it into a bunker. Or even fails to move it more than a couple of yards. What could be more infuriating—and more insulting—than that!

The fact that you can do ninety-nine things right in a golf stroke and only one little insignificant thing wrong, with a result that amounts to complete failure, lives always with us. Nothing is more irrevocably the motto of every golfer—from Open Champion down to beginner—than the old one that 'it is human to err'. The calibre of the golfer shows in how gracefully and philosophically he accepts this fact.

Open Champions never win without half a dozen strokes—often perhaps a score—which they would heartily like to have been able to play over again. Great men hit the merest foozles. Perhaps that makes it all the merrier.

The really great player is the one who can accept the error when it is made—whether it be from judgement, from bad striking, or from sheer inattention—and go on to the next stroke with an unaffected mind. It is all a matter of character, philosophy, and a sense of proportion.

It is perhaps a measure of how potentially devastating this game is that in writing the above paragraphs I have felt my own gorge rising with irritation at my own pomposity. The most irritating thing about them is that they are true. And the reason that I, sir, and you, sir (or you, madam), suffer all alike is not only in our swings but in ourselves.

The professionals and the greater amateurs will nearly all tell you that the first essential in competitive play is never to carry the mood of that bad shot up the fairway with you and wrap it into the next stroke—thus destroying mental equilibrium and spoiling another. When you see a professional banging the ground with his club in a tournament, you can suspect that he is finished: for that one, anyway.

The same doesn't always go for amateurs, since amateurs have —or should have—a more free-and-easy attitude to the game, and the wounds they inflict upon their egos by their inepter performances are never as serious as a professional's are to him. He is playing his career and his future and his living (and that of his family). The amateur is playing for his interest and his pride and just to show that wretched ball who's meant to be in charge!

But for both alike, in fact for every golfing one of us, rage is one of the two great handicaps to good golf. It will hit you in ways that, on reflection, look quite absurd. Take, for instance, the club week-end golfer, having a go at the monthly medal. He has a good start, for a change, and is the equivalent of two strokes under his handicap after five holes. He is in fact coasting along nicely, and only needs to continue to do so in order to come in with a really good score—for him. This he feels quite confident of achieving. In fact, he gets as far as wondering vaguely how on earth he usually finds the game so much more difficult. Today anyway he is at last playing what he considers, nay, what he *knows*, to be his normal game.

Off the 6th tee, he cheerfully and confidently bangs away a nice long drive; with just a trace of slice on it perhaps; and as it lands it hits a hard lump, bounces sharply to the right, and capers away across the fairway, to enter the edge of the rough with its very last turn. When he gets there he finds it nestling in somebody else's large divot hole, with a nasty little baby gorse bush pushing up behind it. Twelve inches less run, and he'd have had a clear bang for the green. But now, instead, all he can do is to take a hack. Annoyed, he gets the ball out, too rashly, and it runs into the cross rough, or a bunker further up. He ends up with a 7.

He tells himself, or tries to tell himself, that after·all he's still doing well, being level with his handicap—and that he often takes 6 at that last hole anyway!

But, try as he may, the sheer injustice of it catches at him. It *wasn't* a bad drive at all. It didn't deserve that lie. If only the greenkeepers would, etc., etc. . . . ! Before he knows what has happened to him he's taken another 7, or else begun to three-putt on green after green. His good day is gone; the game is just as difficult as it always was; and he is by now cursing harder and harder or making hard-pressed (and much-too-late) attempts to be philosophical.

If he'd accepted that bad break-shot philosophically, he'd in all probability have got his 5 at the 6th—and have gone on to complete a pleasing round.

Temperament, of course, is not in any way to be denied. And the type of golfer who rages inwardly at his own stupidity, but *not* at the bad luck that attends it or the greenkeeping that abets it, is a different character. There is little hope for him, honest and forceful character that he is. He may (especially if strictly brought up and wholeheartedly believing in the older-fashioned system of behaviour) contrive to hold both his tongue and his limbs in check. But the rage builds up inside him. Within a few holes he is playing worse than ever and proceeding into a stage of cold, controlled, inhibited, self-condemnatory fury which is bad for his blood pressure, ruinous to his score, and rather frightening for any fairly perceptive golfer who happens to be playing with him.

So what is the answer?

I suggest this: Blame yourself for your bad shots, as enthusiastically as you like; but never believe they really represent you! Explode if you must, but do so at once, with dignity and with style. Bad language is satisfying in a way, but tends to raise a slight subconscious embarrassment. *Anything that makes you feel any whit less of a proper golfer and a level-headed one, will take its toll in strokes.* Having exclaimed and maybe (if, but only if, in the rough—never on the fairway) thumped the ground with your club if you must—forget it and brighten up. Address yourself to the next shot with a completely fresh mind; and with fully renewed confidence that *you play the game to enjoy yourself*, and you enjoy hitting *good* shots, and so you certainly intend to hit some. Then do, and the whole affair is over.

You could sum it up by saying: 'Rage is inevitable—but let us as least relax.'

A few deep breaths can help. So can a hymn tune resolutely hummed. Or any other sort of tune. So can a pipe or cigarette. So can anything that you personally find helps to return you as quickly as possible to a state of cheerful equilibrium: even if it's breaking all your clubs across your trolley and jumping on your umbrella (though this may get you something of a reputation).

## 2. Tendency to disappointment

Rage is better than this. This is fatal. How you fight it, I don't know. But beat it you must, or you will never realize your best potentialities as a golfer.

This, you thought, was going to be your day. It started badly. After two holes you already have the beginning of a millstone round your neck. You begin to *expect* trouble, and find it. You begin to anticipate missing every possible putt—and miss them. It really is quite amazing how a succession of holes can then be played without a single really bad shot, and strokes be lost at each and every one of them!

The same thing goes even more so in match-play. You are three up, or even four up, and then your opponent begins to play brilliantly, or brings off a couple of palpable flukes; and before you know where you are you are brought back to square. Life becomes once more a difficult struggle; and you feel things are flowing unfairly against you. You anticipate more trouble. It comes.

The antidote to both of these is just character, or resolution. It is in the nature of golf that rubs of the green daunt the player in his happiest as well as his most wretched moments. But a player discouraged is almost always a player lost. As with rage, the art of golf in this department is to accept things as they come, and play on regardless. Relax. It's a good game still.

It's difficult. But it can be done, as any good player will tell you.

The psychology is different in medal-play from match-play. In medal-play there is nothing in the world going to affect how you come out in the end except yourself. Aim at the best score which still remains reasonably possible to you, and play out for it determinedly. *Expect* the luck of things to balance out: if they went wrong to begin with, well then they can come right to end with.

In match-play, the ploy is to remember that your opponent is human too. Put in a quick hard blow, a resolute thrust, and he'll be disappointed too—especially when he has just got back to square. It is amazing the number of matches that are saved at the 17th or 18th—after one player has been down all the way—and then lost, by the man who had recovered, at the 18th, 19th, or 20th. It happens.

It may be exhausting to lose four holes in a row, but it was also exhausting for the other chap to win them—or it should have been, if you were hanging on hard.

### 3. The repeating inevitable

It may be a slice, hook, top, cut, foozle, push, pull, or any of the particular ills to which a player's game may be subject.

You get 'em. You begin to think, not: 'Here's a fairway—let's belt this ball up the middle of it' but: 'Here's a fairway with a line of bunkers on the left. Oh heck; one more hook and I'm in them.' And you are.

Thinking does it—just as much as any fault in the swing. If the tendency is there, because something in the method is slightly out of gear, then expecting it will make it worse with absolute certainty. It is far more likely, though, that the first slice or hook was really just one of those accidents of play; and that *the rest have begun in your mind, rather than in your body*.

Nothing, in this situation, is more fatal than trying to 'play pawky'. The more you hold back, the more you'll do whatever it is you are afraid of doing. The rule is to be 'bloody, bold, and resolute' and let fly in your most majestic style.

If it *does* happen again, then there's probably some good reason for it; and if you have at some time mastered the method of producing at will (however inconsistently) whatever type of bad shot you are now doing by accident, then at least you will have some idea how to correct it. Stop and think. Take a few practice swings including the correction, and then let fly at the next with confidence again.

If it still goes on, you must play to allow for it—a very second-best precaution, this—and on return to the clubhouse hie you to the professional. It may be that he can spot what is causing the trouble in two minutes, and put you right. He may be too busy to deal with you at that moment, and only offer you a lesson at a future date.

But if the thing is happening consistently, then either you ask him to help you, or you go to the practice ground and strive to do the opposite fault until you have things straightened out.

This is, for most people, a difficult and chancy remedy. But it is also fun—and sessions of it pay any player in the end (however much he may still be well advised to call in the professional's help).

Remember though: the thing *is* in the mind. Nothing makes a bunker more magnetic than the fear of it. Consider it not. Play for the top of the fairway or the top of the pin.

## 4. Terror on the putting green

I don't know the answer to this one. If I did, I'd be quite a capable performer. See chapter on putting. Pray if you feel so inclined.

The only other remedy is practice. If you have time for it, and don't suffer too much from any tendency to lumbago, try it.

Often the mere thought of relaxing and relying on instinct alone can work wonders. I have known players whose putting problems were solved when they just decided *never to think about putting again*, to consign all considerations of method or technique to the tiger country, and just walk up to every putt and hit it at the hole as naturally as a small boy at a fairground. They are lucky. You may be one of them.

Oh, and by the way, you'll never play your best golf without believing you're a much better player than everyone else thinks you are (even perhaps than you are!). Just as you may never in your life consistently achieve your best physically potential game, so is it true that the potertial is there: even if only for you, perhaps in vague golfing dreams, has it any finite reality.

One plays towards it; and neither hope nor illusion ever really fades—thank goodness!

Meanwhile, if you seem to be shying at the very sight of the hole, it's as well to make sure that your trouble isn't one of the simple ones given in the next chapter.

# 23

# Putting check-points

### Twelve ways of missing short putts

1. *Trust to luck*. Go at it too quickly—and fail to hole it; because—although you hit it exactly as you meant to—you hadn't been careful enough to sum up the subtleties of the putt.

2. *Freezing on it*. Look at it so long and so hard that by the time you come to hit it you are so tensed up that the result is only a convulsive lurch of the hands. It is no good knowing exactly how you guess the ball will run, if in the process of finding out you render yourself incapable of striking it properly. The best advice here is to make sure you utterly dissociate the two parts of the putting drill.

*First* weigh up the strength and line needed; and do not get down to the putt until you have *definitely* decided how you intend to strike it. Then, once you get down to the putt, give considerations of line and strength no further thought—save to follow your own orders for the stroke. You can't be right every time in your judgement, nor can you always hit it exactly as you mean to.

But, while thus being somewhat philosophical in your approach, remember that a short putt 90 per cent correctly estimated and 90 per cent correctly struck will go down 90 per cent of the time—or more!

3. *Funk*. Be afraid you are going to miss it—as you did the one on the last green—and miss it you will. And the next, and the next!

Each putt is a separate and entirely new problem. Nothing that happened last time can affect it at all—*except via the brain*.

4. *Looking up*. If you look up to see how the ball is going before you have hit it, you will make yourself that much more likely to jerk the ball off line. Either look at the ground where the ball was before you hit it, or follow the putter-head through with your eye until it stops. Then look up to see the ball into the hole.

5. *Turning the blade over*. Vastly more short putts are missed on the left of the hole than on the right. This is because in nearly every other shot in the game the hands work towards the left as you hit the ball. So they try to do that on the putt as well, and the result is the face turning to the left as you hit the ball, just enough to send it left of the hole, or to put enough hook on it to make it turn off the line of its own accord.

Push the *heel* of the club also through towards the hole, and this can't happen.

6. *Tensing up*. Whatever happens, one must try to eliminate all external considerations from the putting stroke. Whether you have: This to win, or to save the match, This for a 6 that will otherwise be a 7, or This for the Open—all that side of the matter is irrelevant, and consciousness of it will not help you one whit to hole the putt.

Your left hand can be as tight as you like—but no external considerations must get themselves under the skin of the right, the 'touch' the 'holing' hand. Unless it is relaxed and happy in its little job, the muscles just cannot direct the ball naturally. If it quavers, get up, flex your hands; and get straight into the stroke again.

(There is a contrary theory that whatever the occasion, if it matters to the player, tension is inevitable; therefore, tension must be accepted, and the whole putting movement of both hands must be one of controlled tension. Well, try it. It may suit you better, but it can be much harder work. For a good exposition of this theory, see 'Pressure Putting,' by John Jacobs, *Golfing*, July 1959.)

7. *Dying on the stroke.* This is a disease to which 'strike-and-stop' players are particularly prone. It manifests itself in a just-too-long back-swing, slowing down cravenly as it comes into the ball. The result is a feebly struck putt, which is darned lucky if it reaches the hole at all. This disease often goes in hellish league with a tendency to *jab down* on the putt, making it jump, bobble, and squirm on its way. This is the poor relation of the 'hit-firmly-down-through-it' type of putting—and a pretty poor relation it is too! A weak jab after a long back-swing is about the most unreliable putting method there is.

8. *Leaving it short.* This, to a non-golfer, sounds impossible—that a growing man, having carefully worked out the line and everything for a crucial putt, and then hitting it dead on the line he intends to, somehow forgets to hit it hard enough to reach the hole. But it happens. It happens particularly to people with a tendency to 'joily' the ball in. The best insurance against this most morale-destroying of all methods of missing short putts is to make it part of your putting drill to give the ball at least six inches of run through the centre of the hole.

With this, there is some slight chance of a rimming putt failing to drop; but the comparative dangers of rimming past and putting short are something each player must work out for himself, in the light of his own method, temperament, and the sort of green he is putting on.

One rule: the cleaner the edge of the hole, the safer the firm putt becomes, from the purely mechanical point of view of catching the inside edge firmly.

9. *Jumping it out of the back.* A rare fault this, coming from the

overbold stroke. However firmly a ball hits the back of the hole, it will not drop down into it if its momentum is so great that over half the ball is still above the surface of the ground when it reaches the back of the rim. And if it hits any part of the rim but the exact right angle at the back, then it will certainly tend to climb up the side again and out. Aim never to be more than at most eighteen inches past the hole, and you won't jump out at the back, so long as you are somewhere near the centre. R. T. (Bobby) Jones Jnr. always believed in 'the dying ball'. If the ball is just about spent when it reaches the hole, then any connection whatsoever with the inside of the rim will drag it into the hole by simple force of gravity. On fast greens, with a sharp clean edge to the hole, quite a firm putt will go in. On slow, whiskery greens, with soft edges to the hole, beware the overbold putt.

10. *Favouring the borrow.* This is one particularly to beware of. Say you have decided a putt is just outside the left lip. There can then be a tendency, particularly under pressure, to make extra certain that you hit the ball on the borrow side by giving a little twist of the putter-blade that way as you hit it. This, of course, is making nonsense of the whole method, since the aim is to hit the ball dead straight in the line chosen. But the mind will have its leaps and jerks and appetites for over-reassurance— and can push you into a hook, or shove, outside the borrow-line before you know what is happening to you.

11. *Helping the borrow.* This is probably one of the most insidious of all potent putting faults. The more especially since it is so often completely unrecognized, and then elicits a simple 'hard luck' impression in both player and spectator—particularly amongst week-end golfers.

It consists in quite the most simple and human thing in the world. Having worked out accurately a borrow of some twelve inches on a ten-foot putt, the player then addresses the ball with a crystal-clear picture of the putt's path in his head—and strikes it in such a way as to *assist* the ball to produce that path! If the borrow is from the left, then he delicately puts a shade of cut on the ball; if it is from the right, then he equally delicately pushes the toe through the shot just enough to start it off with a little hook stored up in it.

**The** result is nearly always a putt that just misses the hole on 'the amateur side', and leaves the player feeling that he honestly underestimated the borrow.

This can happen in its most damaging—and least perceptible —form on the really short ones. Just think how many times you have missed a two-and-a-half-foot putt by aiming at the right lip, and curling out of the left lip! At least five times in ten, this sort of miss comes about through 'helping the borrow'.

How to guard against it, I just don't know—especially as the player in the habit of doing it often instinctively corrects it by giving the putt a little bit of extra borrow as well, and holes a fair proportion of them!

In theory, the answer is, of course, to aim straight at an imaginary hole in the middle of your line of aim, and strike the ball dead at it.

If you consistently miss putts on the amateur side, suspect that you may be 'helping the borrow'.

12. '*Looking up*'. Not really up, of course, but beginning to move your eyes along the path towards the hole just as your blade is coming into the ball. The result may be a perfectly good putt, and often will be for some weeks after you have acquired this habit.

Then suddenly everything will begin to feel doubtful; and putt after putt, hit not quite truly, will puzzle you by its behaviour.

Develop an interest in the grass directly under the ball, and after the ball is struck, take a look at it, before you move your eye.

Some players, particularly on short putts, have putted well with their eye fixed on the hole instead of the ball (rather as a pistol-shooter looks at the target and fires by instinct). If ever *in extremis*, it may be worth trying.

The above examples are probably more than enough to make putting sound almost impossible to the beginner, and to remind the more experienced player of all too many unhappy occasions in his career. So it's as well to remember, also, that hardly anything in the world is really quite so simple as knocking a little ball straight into a large hole from four feet away. Auntie could do it with her umbrella. It's just the thinking that makes it difficult.

Successful golf is less a matter of achieving the difficult, than of avoiding the fatuous.

**Note to all putting**

The flagstick. *Take it out or have it attended.* More putts are missed by hitting it than are ever missed by jumping out of the side or back.

There are players, though, who argue that this is more than balanced out by the fact that, with the precise centre-mark of the stick to aim at, they hit the hole far more often than they do with the stick out; and that, despite missing some through hitting the stick, they still hole more putts than they would if aiming at an empty tin. How they use this as a logical argument against having a stick attended, I have never quite been able to understand. But they do.

The mind of a golfer is always a rule unto itself; and believing is achieving.


# 24

# The tactics of recovery play

**Rule 1—It's hardly ever impossible!**

This statement and its implications are almost completely in dispute with the advice usually given to amateurs by professionals, and by some older players, which is: pick up and cut your losses, accepting the two strokes, or stroke and distance, penalty.

My own impression is that most players who pick out, when they could have hacked a ball out somehow, do not cut their losses at all. They go back and play another bad shot; and the loss is doubled!

There is also the basic tradition of the game, which is that the ball should be played as it lies. It is up to you to manufacture your own techniques to enable you to do so whenever humanly possible.

*Much better, and more correct, to take two hacks to remove a ball from thickage, and put it up the fairway, than to go back to the tee and drive another into trouble.*

The first aim, in all recovery shots, should be to get length if it is at all possible. So long as you can bring the club-face into the ball, or the cutting edge of the club into the ground under and through the ball—the darned thing will move! If you can be sure it will move into a playable position, then the shot is worth the attempt.

This is the proper interpretation of the rules. But if you are only going to succeed in lobbing the ball straight into a clump of gorse bushes, a pond, or out of bounds—then the modern custom of allowing a wide and quite unliteral interpretation of 'The player shall be the sole judge of whether he can dislodge the ball into a playable position', allows you to pick it out and play safe.

In all this, looking ahead is essential tactics. If, with a hack and then another hack, you can be confident of gaining 50 to 100 yards on the distance of a normal good shot, from wherever you played the bad one, then this gives you an advantage over going back and playing a second—even if you hit it perfectly.

In general, there is one thing that should be borne in the mind *as a fact*. In trouble from the tee: hack it out successfully, and then be playing a shorter 3rd shot than will be your 4th if you pick up and go back to the tee. You ought to get a 5; you may make a 4—out of sheer relief at not having lost 2 strokes already. But take it back and you are aiming at a 6 from the word go—a 6 which is very likely to become a 7.

### Seize the best chance

Not so very long ago, my wife found herself playing in a friendly club match against a woman she had not met before. Although her opponent had not been playing the game for long, she was obviously a natural player and likely to make quite a good golfer

by ordinary standards before much longer. This made it all
the more puzzling that, whenever she went off the fairway at all,
out came her niblick; and she calmly played the ball about
thirty yards up the fairway, whatever the lie and whatever the
distance she needed. It transpired that her professional had told
her that the proper thing to do when in the rough was to make
sure of getting out, had taught her how to do so quietly and
sensibly with a niblick—and the dear lady had somehow got it
into her head that whenever she was in the rough that was the
club she was supposed to take and that was the way she was
supposed to play it! A fine example of excellent advice too
literally interpreted!

Playing the longer shots out of the rough is what separates the
tiger from the rabbit. It is remarkable how many golfers, to the
end of their days, cherish the same attitude to rough play as my
wife's opponent did. There is an understandable reason for this.
For the player who is either not very strong, or not very much
appraised of the various methods possible for recovery shots,
any attempt to play a long iron from any but the luckiest of lies,
tends to lead to a fluff.

This won't apply to anyone working on the principles in
Chapter 12. But there remain dangers, especially in trying to use
one club too low; and here is one point at which the usual professional's habitual advice to the club golfer: 'Make sure of
getting out,' is nothing but wisdom. Out of bad rough a 4-iron
will give you maybe five to seven yards more length than a 5-iron
—if properly hit. Much more likely it will not be quite properly
hit and will give you less length than the same stroke attempted
with a 5-iron. Often it will simply fail to remove the ball, and
you'll stay where you are.

For the average player, the best approach where the most
length is wanted is something like this: 'Can I certainly hit it
well with a 7-iron?' '*Yes*'. 'Well, can I get a 4-wood to it well
enough away to send it as far as a 5-iron?' If the answer to that is
*no*, then almost certainly a 3- or 4-iron will be impossible too,
and possibly a 5-iron as well. In the old days of more practically
designed clubs, this didn't apply. But with to-day's almost
universal straight-bottomed iron clubs, for any but the strongest

player, when going for length out of a doubtful lie in the rough, it must be either a spoon or a 4-wood, or a 5- or 6-iron—and *nothing in between.*

This is because spoons are still made with a reasonably curved and compact cutting edge, and often with something of a downward bite to them. They can thus get the ball up out of thick stuff much more easily than a straight-edged 4-iron. Both the cut-up shot and the toe-first hook can be used more easily with a spoon; and, with the grip held firmly and the swing cut down a bit, can send the ball just about the length of a 3-iron.

In still worse lies, the question to ask is simply: 'How easily can I get the face of which club to it?' It is the *club-face* that is going to do the job. Has it a chance? If you have got to 'hit up at it' with the club you choose before it will safely rise clear of the trouble, then you have almost certainly chosen the wrong club. Take a shorter one, and hit through it!

But again, as with all awkward shots, craftsmanship is the determining factor, both in choice of stroke and in execution. What you can do on the course will be decided by what you have been able to teach yourself, and make yourself a fair master of in practice and experiment.

The best sense in which to read the universal 'play safe' advice which will be offered you is this: 'If *in doubt*, get out.'[1]

[1] Wherever and whenever the present two-stroke penalty for picking out is reduced to only one stroke—then the whole basis of the above chapter will be changed; for there will be then a much greater premium on not taking risks which could cost you twice the penalty of picking out and dropping behind.

# 25

# Tactics in medal play

Golf is not just hitting a ball; it is looking ahead.

We have already dealt with the absolutely fatal psychological and practical error of looking back at the shots already played—a human and natural weakness which has produced more runs of bad holes, and more disappointments after a good start, than any other in golf. But the thing to notice at this stage is that looking back like that is not just an error in practical thinking and shot-making; it is an error in tactics.

*What counts is what comes next.*

Perhaps my best plan would be to divide tactics into two separate compartments—medal play and match play. And to make things simple, let's set aside for the moment any considerations of how well you are doing (or feeling), and what sort of weather you are having, and address the problem purely as one of playing the course.

**Medal play: It's the total that counts**
The first and overriding tactic in medal play is to get away to a good start.

It is the greatest help in the world to set off in a relaxed state of mind, but an intelligently concentrating one. Too cheerful a 'Well, here we go' spirit can lead inexorably to a dropping of strokes in the first two holes. Too dour a 'Now for the serious business' one can have a very similar effect; for any player of normal temperament will be slightly strung up at the beginning of a medal round, and to add too ferocious a determination to that given state tends to *produce* a certain inhibition in striking. Relax and let fly, but think first what you intend to do.

Every tee shot—including the first—should be approached very much from the point of view of what sort of second shot you want to play. It is begging for trouble to bang off cheerfully at the middle of the first fairway, find you have given it a bit of hook, and end up with a nasty angled shot close to some trees and over a bunker for your first iron shot of the day.

Much better to stop and think and even—if the length allows —place a 2-iron down on whichever side of the fairway will give you the easiest approach to the green. If the hole is a long one, you may even have to think more of where you want to place your long second shot, and the best angle from which to play it. Often the mere length of the tee shot is much less important than the line on which it finishes. Much easier to play a 5-iron to an open green, than to play a 7-iron at an awkward—and frightening—angle.

This policy can, of course, be modified. If you find you are driving well, then you can sometimes go all-out for length, in the ambition of playing as short as possible a shot to the green and hoping to get close enough to hole the putt; or at least to get your second shot close enough to the green to be able to get down in a chip and a putt (depending on the length of the hole and the degree of proficiency you have reached in the game).

In medal-play, though, it is often a fact that you pick up more strokes—or lose fewer—by playing the hole the straightforward way, than you do by attempting to seize an advantage by sheer valour. This is depressing and boring, and against fun, but it is true. Two quiet shots and then a poke-up for a safe 5 will often bring a putt for 4—which you hole confidently; whereas two great beats—your very best, successfully brought off—often leave a chip or a long putt which does not quite go close enough and leaves a similar-length putt which suddenly becomes difficult, simply because you are no longer in the position of seizing a stroke by practical achievement, but in danger of throwing away the one you have all but seized already.

In medal play, patience is a golden virtue.

Now for the exactly opposite proposition, just to underline what a contrary game golf is! The player who sets out to play the holes quietly and safely all too often ends up by getting a sad and undignified 6, instead of a safe 5. The second shot becomes pawky, the third all too 'safe', at the very front of the green, and three putts follow! There are really pretty wide generalities in golf—for much depends on the player's own temperament and feelings. And the bold player can, and will, always argue with justification that, even if his two great slashes didn't earn him a 4, they made a 5 pretty easy!

Are you, in fact, by temperament a 'slasher' or a 'sneaker'? If you quail at the sight of a four-foot putt, then boldness will often pay you; but if you look on a six-foot putt as just a matter of hitting the ball calmly into the hole, then your calm 5 will often turn out to be a 4.

*Your own tactics must depend very largely upon your own temperament.*

There are, though, some admirable general rules. First of them is:

### Which side of the green?

Let's assume for this section that your chipping is fairly reliable —however you feel about the short putts. How do you then approach the shot to the green?

Now, on nearly every green in golf, there is *for you personally* a safest quarter to play for. Often it will be the back area of the green—for many courses set their bunkers more to catch the weak and off-line shot than to trap the shot which pitches at the back. Look at the green.

If all the bunkers are pin-high, or less than pin-high, and the rough over the back is fairly short semi-rough—then give the shot that extra strength. Two shots identical for line, both with the same amount of slight cut on them, will, at this hole, meet different deserts according to their length. The first, which would just have reached the pin if it had stayed straight, will side-step and squirm remorselessly into a bunker; the second, pitching near the pin, will run sideways to exactly the same extent, but end by leaving you a simple chip, or even a putt, from the back.

Or it may be that the pin is placed at the back of the green, and close to a line of bunkers on one side. The intention is to tempt you to go for it; slightly misjudge the line, and find sand. Unless you are a top-class player in the making, you will really do best to go for the middle of the green, or even—if the hazards there are negligible—for the opposite side of the green. It all depends on the contours—which you will know on most courses you play, and which, on any course new to you, you will usually be able to estimate. Often it is much better to have a straight uphill twenty-foot putt, than a curly downhill twelve-footer.

Or say you face a green which offers you this alternative: a very nasty recovery shot if you miss it on one quarter, or a nasty long chip or putt if you miss it on the opposite side. Stop and think: which of these two shots would you be more likely to put within sure holing distance? Then make your choice of tee shot accordingly.

In tournaments you will see many professionals, under extreme pressure, taking what seems to you to be the foolhardy line. But for them it is not, because to them a twenty-foot bunker shot (if the sand is of good consistency) is not very difficult—and they expect to put it near the hole. They will take the risk of having to get a 4 with a bunker shot in the hope of getting a putt for 3. Play the other way—the side that looks wiser to you—and *they* condemn themselves to a 4 before the ball is even hit.

The thing to do is to know your own feelings, always to play to give yourself the sort of approach chip or putt you are confident about, and to avoid the sort of shot which—though it may be easier to other people—is not easy to you.

Nine times out of ten, of course, the ball won't go exactly where you meant it to. But at least, if the shot was reasonably struck, it is likely to give you the general type of next shot you selected.

If, however, there is one rule for the week-end golfer which tends in practice to overweigh all others in approaching a green, it is that mentioned above in passing—*be up*. The shot that ends *plus* of the pin leaves you more confident, and very often far closer to your target, than the shot that erred towards caution.

Remember, too, a mishit bold shot gets somewhere 'thereabouts'. A mishit pawky one gets nowhere. And a tremendous number of your shots—even when you become a low-handicap player—are going to be slightly mishit!

# 26

# Tactics in match play

The first requisite of all tactics in match play is to show your opponent no sign of weakness.

You may be two down and scared stiff that you are going to top the next one into the cross-bunker; but for heaven's sake don't let him see it.

Nothing is more perturbing to a player—so far as anything *can* be in the situation—than to observe that his opponent, who is three down (or even more) appears to be not one whit worried about it. I have countless times seen the scrupulous observance of this rule enable players to be given back matches which, on the basis of normal play, they had already completely and irrevocably lost.

What happens is that if the man who is down keeps on playing imperturbably, *and cheerfully*, he is likely to produce a hole-winning stroke and get one back, whereupon it is difficult for his opponent not to find the thought flashing through his mind: 'Hm! He obviously knew that was coming. What else has he on the way?'

It seems quite childlike and unworthy of grown men! But that is the way many golfers' minds work in match play, since there is always—up or down—a substratum of anxiety.

Never forget to take this into account.

And now let us categorize under two headings:

**How to help your opponent to win**

1. Show him that you are hurt or perturbed when he wins a hole.

2. Take three putts, or otherwise give him a hole he thought he was going to halve or even lose. Try never to take three putts in match-play—nothing encourages your opponent more.

3. If you are two or three up, get over-confident. He will spot this. Either it will encourage him to think you are about to do

something careless (which you are); or else he will feel it an insult to his manliness, and of a sudden resolve furiously to do you, if it's the last thing on earth he achieves. Strangely, this will often have a remarkably good effect upon his game!

4. Mutter about how you played a silly stroke as you walk to the next tee. He will listen most sympathetically (if he knows his tactics), and slip a few commiserative philosophic remarks. 'Just goes that way sometimes, doesn't it?'—leaving you to continue with that in mind. (This is not gamesmanship; this is just politeness.)

5. Let him see that you are frantically keen to win, or otherwise alienate his sympathies from you as a chap to play golf with. If he decides he doesn't like you, then he'll be all the more cold and resolute in his resolve.

### How to help your opponent to lose

1. Start well and keep going. This may give you a lead of a hole or so. But do not expect to hold it automatically. Expect him to play some admirable shots and get a hole or two back. Look on an early lead merely as a useful insurance policy.

2. If you are capable of doing so without spoiling your own concentration, play your shots a little more quickly and care-freely than he does. This applies particularly if you are a hole or so up. Leave him to exhaust himself with excessive concentration, if he will. Often he will.

3. Be bold always, or almost always. In match-play it pays. But when two up or more, you can risk playing a tricky hole particularly safely. If he happens to do something silly, and lose it to you, the pyschological effect is that much greater.

4. Never give up. *Never* give up. Even if he is winning easily, make him work every shot of the way to the end. At worst, you may cut down the margin to a minumim. At best, you may stick it out till he suddenly starts to slide—and, before he quite knows how it has happened, you have him.

5. Pay particular attention to your approach to the next hole after one or the other of you has squared the match. If this is late in the round, the result of this one hole can be decisive. Pause a moment mentally before you come to the tee, and think

out how you intend to play it. Then swing away confidently and do so. You thus offer him an opportunity to lose it, which he is always likely to take.

6. You may appreciate his good shots quietly and frankly, whenever they really deserve it. But watch it. There are occasional golfers who cherish an instinctive hostility for any opponent on principle. They make excellent match-players.

7. Nearly all the rest of the general tactics under this heading verge very closely on gamesmanship.[1]

### Practical match play

This can differ most radically from medal play in actual striking tactics. It will take you a hole or two to sum up your man, even if he is someone you have often played with; since his form on any one day may be variable.

Then, from hole to hole, anticipate, if you can, what he is likely to do, and set your own targets accordingly.

But don't overdo it. My own feeling is that the best of all match play general tactics is to play it as a medal.

Obviously this will not always apply at particular holes. If he has put a tremendously rash or brilliant stroke on the green, then you must aim to be thereabouts in the like number; and playing medal will not get you anywhere. If, on the other hand, he has gone out of bounds, or is obviously going to take a 6, and you have only played 1, then go for the safest approach to the green: no reason why you shouldn't take three putts if you have them!

If losing a hole, never throw it at him. Always aim to play out and force him to *actually win it*. He may find himself with two putts for the hole—and find them rather difficult! If he gets duly down, you have still put him to the pressure of doing so; and every little helps.

Always believe he has some bad holes coming to him. If he hasn't: fair enough!

If he looks like having a three-foot putt for a win, never be short with your longer one—but don't overrun and take three putts. Make him have to hole it.

[1] See: *Gamesmanship: The Art of Winning Games Without Actually Cheating*, by Stephen Potter. And beware.

# 27

# Never give up

'When I am 9 down, I strive to be 8 down!'

I'm likely to be a bit of a bore on this subject particularly, being of the type of golfer who has hardly ever achieved any minor success easily, and who has gained a very fair share of the reliefs that can come to a man who has made things difficult for himself by a few bad holes, yet hacks on in stupid and incorrigible optimism.

Optimism isn't really quite as stupid as all that. Even on the very highest levels of the game, the impossible sometimes becomes fact. (Echoing somewhere behind this sentence the apocryphal verdict of one of those much-quoted old Scottish professionals: 'It's no possible. But it's a fact.') And in the lower levels of the game, where the beginner inevitably starts, and in which even many comparatively outstanding performers amongst men spend the whole of their recreational lives, the impossible is much more common.

To take an example or two, beginning at the lowest level, I always remember one in particular, as not only one of the most outstandingly absurd but as one with the clearest of possible morals. In a golfing society to which I belong, I made up a single one day with a young man who had turned up for our autumn meeting, whom I had never met before. As it happened that year, one of the doyens of the society had presented an old trophy of his, won many many years before in the China Station, for annual medal competition between those still under twenty-six years of age. My fellow player was one of these. Berkhamsted is a difficult course; it was a windy gusty day; and my young friend had a fantastically terrible round (even, he said, for him). Finally he came to a position halfway up the 16th in some 15 strokes from the tee and was obviously about to pick up his ball.

We had a long argument, I insisting that I was still marking his card, he insisting that he was giving up. In the end I won. He removed the ball from the bush with three angry hacks, and eventually holed it right across the green to be down in 19; 12 at the 17th and 9 at the 18th gave him a total beyond my possible recall, but I still persuaded him to countersign the card. Later it proved that every single other competitor for the Rice Cup had torn up his card in fury; and my man, left alone in the field, went home unopposed with the finest pot he is ever likely to hold in his golfing life.

He was rather embarrassed, but extremely pleased.

My own name is on one of the club boards as having won the winter Scratch Medal once or twice. What the board doesn't say is that the first time it came my way it followed a score of 91! It was another of Berkhamsted's wet blustery days. I was out in 53 and laboured home in 38, thoroughly soaked—to find that the next-best card was 93. I have seen a man reach the semi-final of my local county championship merely because, when he was 4 down with 6 to play, his unfortunate opponent endured in successive holes: one unplayable lie, three putts, a shank, a 2 against him, and then another shank—and lost on the last green, which he halved, very valiantly in the circumstances, in 4. It was the most completely unforeseeable turn of fortune, but typical of golf.

Moving now up the scale to class golf, M. S. R. Lunt, then not even a Walker Cup probable, took a horrible 8 on an early hole on the Old in the *Golf Illustrated* Gold Vase at Sunningdale, in 1958. He also suffered on several greens. But he kept on trying, somehow returning a card in the middle seventies—and then in the afternoon found everything coming right for him. He sailed round the New course in 65 to win the Vase, and take—as it proved—an invaluable step towards getting into the Walker Cup team.

For one more example (and four is enough), take again Fred Bullock, who came nearest of any British player to holding off Gary Player in the 1959 Open at Muirfield. When he had dropped a number of strokes through putting in the morning of the final day, had begun in the afternoon with two fives in the first three holes and then drove into an unplayable lie in a bunker at the 5th, the minority who had still thought that he had a chance reckoned that that was emphatically that. Nevertheless, two hours later, there he was on the 18th tee needing a quite-possible 3 to tie! One of the most determined performances ever seen of a man hanging valiantly on to his chances—no matter what the vast majority of pundits thought about them!

The repetition may become boring; but it really is a prime lesson to be learnt in this game. You will always hit a number of bad shots in a round—or nearly always—and you will often pay for them. But it can turn out sometimes that they are not all spread evenly throughout the eighteen holes, but concentrated at the beginning.

It is always a rather strange thing about golf that, although a man who has played fourteen holes really well is never surprised if he makes a mess of three of the last four, a man who makes a mess of three of the *first* four hardly ever imagines that he may then play the remaining fifteen really well. Yet sometimes he could, and sometimes he does.

Were it not, in fact, for the usual effect of rage and discouragement in medal-play, it is my belief that the latter pattern would be more common than the former; since it is the commonest thing in the world for a week-end golfer to start with a few loose shots (simply through not having warmed up first on the practice ground), and then to hit everything fairly well, for him, for the rest of the round. He doesn't often score well, because, reckoning that he's already messed everything up, he makes no particular attempt to concentrate on getting down in the right figures, but looks upon the remainder as just a walk with golfing exercises. The mug!

Another point to note about never-give-up-manship is that it applies just as strongly to individual holes as it does to whole rounds, or whole tournaments. You may drive into the tripe, lose the ball, go out of bounds, or foozle a shot (or even two) completely. But if you go valiantly for the green in the end, you stand *as good a chance as at any other time* (in fact, if you are so enraged as to cast all inhibitions aside, slightly better) of putting the long shot not too far away and holing the putt. A lost ball from the tee can—with determination—often lead to a 5 going down on the card at a par 4 (or even a par 5) hole—which counts exactly the same as if you had put two good shots through the green and not quite managed to get the chip close enough.

The psychological effect of such a recovery—in medal or match play alike—is such that a string of well-played holes often follows it! However badly you may have started, or suffered, there is *always* a nice long streak of your very best and luckiest form stored up in the locker for you some time; and now may be the moment when it will suddenly come tumbling out.

Need one, I wonder, in particular stress the 'make-him-do-it' policy once more?

When you are 3 down with 3 to play, you have not lost, nor has your opponent won. You have only to hole one putt, and then he has only to play a single loose shot at the next, for you to come to the 18th tee only 1 down—and who is then going to be in the more confident frame of mind?

# 28

# The enjoyment of golf

I believe that golf is the most fascinating, the most infuriating, and the most rewarding game on earth.

It is fascinating above all in that every single player can produce a number of shots of equal perfection to the Open Champion's—and get a much vaster joy out of them. It is fascinating because it absorbs the mind: it is impossible to think really seriously or consecutively about anything else while playing a round. The game is a complete mental relief, as well as a physical exercise.

Every man has his own inward dream about his own game, and about what he is really capable of—or would be, if only he had the time and opportunity to practise like a professional. The fact that he never lives up to it tarnishes the perfection of his private ideal not one iota.

Wherever he is, and upon whatever course he is playing, there is never anything to stop him from pausing momentarily to admire the view (so long as no one is waiting behind); and from golf courses can be enjoyed some of the most magnificent prospects on earth. There are the spreads of sea, sand, and cliff, viewed from a sudden dune-top, or the sound and tang of the sea churning up shingle as at Deal, and the smell of the wind wet with salt spray.

Inland there are hills and bracken and heather in all hues and textures. Even on the dullest parkland or meadowland course, there are some prospects of trees and hedgerows which please. And if he is lucky enough to join some club whose course lies upon high or open land, there is, especially, the quiet hour before sunset in which to practise away by himself on a far corner of the course.

I know of no better spot on earth to be than out along our 7th fairway on an autumn evening; with the sun closing down over the further ridges of the Chilterns; the wind making the faintest of sounds in the grasses; and the scattered birch, pine, and beech trees turning into black silhouettes against a green sky. Then, as the light fades, a very yellow moon, and layers of mist in the valleys.

Or, in winter, wet gales and red leaves, turning to frosty afternoons with a crispness underfoot in the rough: and the musty tang of bracken-mould disturbed by a niblick.

Purple passage over! But any man may feel the same about the course he settles down to make his own.

Golf can, in fact, introduce a man to an almost limitless variety of pleasures, satisfactions, and interests, in many of the most perfect of settings, and in company unequalled for variety, friendliness, and good-fellowship. To take up the game and join a well-chosen club is to acquire a passport to an ideal recreation, and something of a way of life, which can continually renew itself in interest, and outlast almost any other.